Growing Miracles second edition

Acknowledgements

Growing Miracles has been made possible ⋯ k of a dedicated group of people.

Sincere thanks go to the content specialists from various professions within Alberta Health Services and the Healthy Child and Youth Advisory Committee for their guidance and support. We value the incredible support and continued contributions from our community colleagues to Growing Miracles' second edition. We thank all of you for helping to spread the messages of healthy child development and parenting in your work with parents of young children.

Growing Miracles is funded by Alberta Health Services and that support is gratefully acknowledged.

Finally, thank you to the many parents who reviewed this book and gave us their encouragement, ideas and validation. From choosing the design to pilot testing to helping evaluate the first edition, your input has been invaluable—and is reflected in our redesigned and updated second edition. You have helped us—and all parents—immensely.

Growing Miracles credits:
Writer: **Terry Bullick**
Editor: **Leslie Barker**
Content research: **Alberta Health Services content specialists**
Illustrations: **Leslie Bell**
Graphic Design: **Terry Bullick & Sherry Mumford**
Layout: **Connections Desktop Publishing Ltd.**
Printing: **The DATA Group of Companies**

Table of Contents

Forward

How does a child's mind develop?

As a scientist, researcher and a curious parent, this question is one I've spent much of my adult life trying to answer.

In the simplest of scientific terms, neurons (nerve cells) are the basic building blocks of the brain. Through genes and experience, neurons are connected to other neurons and sculpted to form pathways and networks. These pathways and networks are the foundation for all future learning and make it possible for humans to have the minds needed to create and live in complex, diverse and sustainable communities.

While this process begins in the womb, it dramatically increases after birth. Virtually everything in an infant's world contributes to her brain development—everything she sees, hears, touches, feels, smells or tastes. As her parent, you are the most powerful influence as you create and oversee so many of your child's experiences.

As we learn more about brain development, we're discovering that an infant's brain needs to resonate with other brains in order for the child to develop the capacity to self-regulate. A child's ability to monitor and modify her emotions, pay attention, control her impulses, tolerate frustration, sequence her thoughts and actions—all of these key aspects of self-regulation, and many more, develop in the countless brain-to-brain experiences that occur in the early years of life.

For most children, those other brains are those of their parents. The interaction between parents and their infants is crucial in providing the sensory stimulation and integration needed for healthy brain development.

When this interaction involves broad smiles, loving parentese (the lilting, sing-song language parents speak to their babies), caressing and rocking, it engages infants in trying to respond and helps them to integrate the information coming in from their different senses with their motor system. When a child responds, a parent is encouraged to continue and the cycle goes on—each experience strengthening those early brain connections. This two-way interaction, which needs to be repeated over and over, is at the core of human communication and shapes our ability to think and learn, to form warm and meaningful relationships, and to cope with the stresses of life.

Such parental behaviours are not hardwired. They have been slowly developed and passed down, from one generation to the next, over millions of years. Still, we often engage in these brain-building interactions with our babies without even knowing we are doing so—or recognizing their importance.

Even so, many parents want to better understand these interactions and how they enhance, not just early brain development, but overall early childhood development. Physical, emotional, cognitive and communicative development are all closely linked to early brain development.

Understanding child development takes considerable time, effort and patience—both for scientists and parents. Added to this is the uniqueness of every child: each has developmental strengths and weaknesses and special communication needs. While the differences from child to child can be subtle and slight, they are important and can make a tremendous difference in a child's life.

Growing Miracles does an exceptional job of explaining the foundations of early child development. It gives parents practical, evidence-based information to help them make choices that work for their child and their family.

I believe parents who read and refer often to this book will learn that children's minds develop best with their parents' patience, guidance, love and understanding.

Stuart Shanker
January 2010

Stuart Shanker is a distinguished research professor of philosophy, psychology and education at York University and serves as the director of the Milton and Ethel Harris Research Initiative. Stuart holds a PhD in philosophy from Oxford and was awarded fellowships at the Calgary Institute for the Humanities and the University of Alberta. He is one of the world's foremost experts in early child development and the author and co-author of many books and studies, including *The First Idea* and *Early Years Study 2: Putting Science into Action.*

Introduction

It is a universal truth. Parents around the world want what's best for their children. While they may hope and dream their children will become artists and athletes, farmers and carpenters, doctors and nurses, what they want most is for their children to be healthy, happy adults. More than anything, parents want their children to grow into confident, responsible adults who are able to laugh and smile, care about others and make good choices in their lives.

Like the first edition of *Growing Miracles*, our second edition helps parents—or any adult in a child's life—better understand how to help a child grow and thrive. We believe no other job in the world is as important as being a parent. We want to give parents all the support we can.

No one is born knowing how to be a parent, and no baby is born knowing how to be a child. It's a learning experience for both. While they grow into their roles, children and parents alike can feel supported and influenced—as well as advised and criticized—by the people around them. Never before has there been so much advice about the "best" ways to parent children. *Growing Miracles* will help you balance the many views of parenting with your own knowledge, values, skills and instincts.

Growing Miracles deals with the most important years in child development, from birth to 6 years. During this time, most children learn to crawl, walk, talk and explore the world they live in. They learn to sing, run and share their toys, and what happens when they pull a cat's tail or write on a wall with felt pens. They go from wearing diapers to using toilets, from being toothless to brushing their teeth twice a day.

Children learn more—and learn more naturally—during this time than at any other time in their life. And your child's most important and trusted teacher is you.

Our goal in writing *Growing Miracles* is to help you be a more informed, more confident parent. Parents are always learning. What you learn about being a parent through this book may be different from what you've learned in the past. We've based our information on the best knowledge, evidence and practices of Alberta Health Services.

Growing Miracles is not meant to tell you what to do, but it can help you think about what it means to be a parent and how you can be the parent you want to be.

We looked to many experts for their knowledge and practices in child development and health. We draw from the classic works of John Bowlby, Mary Ainsworth, Abraham Mazlow, Alfred Adler, Eric Erikson, Jean Piaget, and Albert Bandura as well as the more recent works of Drs. Paul Steinhauer, Fraser Mustard, Stuart Shanker, Jack Shonkoff, Bruce Perry, Ronald Barr, Sarah Landy, Joan Durrant, T. Berry Brazelton and Stanley Greenspan. In addition, we include parenting concepts from well-known parenting experts of our day. Among them: Thomas Gordon, Barbara Coloroso, Jane Nelsen, H. Stephen Glenn, Adele Faber and Elaine Mazlich, Laura Davis, Janice Keyser, Elizabeth Crary and Jean I. Clarke. You can find a reading list of these experts' works under *Your Health* at www.healthlinkalberta.ca.

We are especially honoured to have a foreword in our second edition of *Growing Miracles* from Dr. Stuart Shanker of York University.

How this book can help you

In the chapters ahead, you'll find a wealth of information.

Welcome to Parenthood (on page 5) helps you understand your parenting beliefs and style. Whether you are parenting with a partner, on your own or with other family members, this chapter can help you decide what kind of parent you want to be and guide you in your journey.

Miracles in Progress (on page 15) highlights important health, safety and development information for young children of all ages and stages.

The remaining chapters (*Infants, Babies, Toddlers, Preschoolers* and *New Schoolers*) look at how development affects your child at specific ages and stages. Each chapter builds on the one before, and gives you practical ideas for helping your child grow, learn, play and be healthy.

As your child grows, you will also grow as a parent. You will find ideas and tips throughout the book to help you cope with your ever-changing role in the sections called *Caring for you*.

All the information in *Growing Miracles* applies equally to both boys and girls. Throughout the book, we switch back and forth between the pronouns *he* and *she* to indicate this.

Growing Miracles can be read cover to cover, chapter by chapter, or bit by bit. Readers of the first edition told us they reached for it again and again as their children grew. We hope you will too.

When you have questions

Every child and every parent is unique, and every family has different joys and challenges. When you have questions, we can help. Call Health Link Alberta, our toll-free telephone information and advice service. It's available 24 hours a day, seven days a week—all across the province. If you speak a language other than English, just say "I speak (Spanish, Mandarin, Punjabi, Urdu, etc.)" and you will be connected to an interpreter.

Parenting is a joy, but it can also be hard work. You're there to support your children. At Alberta Health Services, we're here to support you.

HEALTHLink Alberta

Health advice 24 hours a day

Toll-free: 1-866-408-LINK (5465)
Calgary: 403-943-LINK (5465)   Edmonton: 780-408-LINK (5465)

WELCOME TO
Parenthood

Congratulations! You're a parent

Now what? You may begin parenthood feeling prepared and confident, but most parents are confused by it at some time. As you enter this new world you may find you have many questions, especially in your children's early years: "Will I be a good parent?" "How can anyone take care of my child as well as I do?" "Why won't my daughter eat her vegetables?", "Does my son have to say no all the time?", "Are my twins ready for school?", "Why does my second child seem so different from my first?"

Whether you are a new parent or have been a parent for several years, this book is for you. It doesn't have all the answers, because parenting is a big job and is always changing. Plus, parenting differs from child to child, parent to parent and from family to family. It can also differ by generation, community, country and culture. How you bring up your child may be quite different from how your parents raised you.

For all its differences, however, effective parenting is based on some very basic approaches:
- Being sensitive and understanding of children's needs,
- Providing warm, nurturing care
- Valuing each child's uniqueness, dignity and worth.

Every parent has questions and all parents need support. This book is a starting point, filled with information you can rely on as you find your own answers and build that support. As you grow into your role as a parent, we hope *Growing Miracles* will help you become more confident and knowledgeable, and that it will help guide you to becoming the parent that you want to be.

Parents and parenting

Defining a parent is not as easy as it seems. Parents might be the birth mother or birth father of a child. People also become parents through adoption, foster care, marriage, new relationships or special circumstances. Some children have extended family members who act as parents—grandparents, aunts, uncles or cousins. How people come to be parents is not as important as the parents they come to be.

The dictionary defines parenting as "the experiences, skills, qualities and responsibilities involved in being a parent and in teaching and caring for a child." In fact, parenting is everything a parent does in raising a child. Although we know more and more about child development and parenting, in practice, parenting is as much an art as a science.

Family life has changed

Today's parents don't always live the same way their parents did 20, 30 and 40 years ago. In North America especially, family life has changed.

Today, families are as unique as the people in them. The so-called "traditional" family—a husband and wife with three or four children—still exists, but is now part of a diverse mix of families, which includes families headed by single parents, step-parents, same-sex parents, foster parents or grandparents. Some families have parents who both work for pay while others have parents who stay at home. Some families are on their own. Other families are huge, with relatives from several generations sharing in their children's care. Still others are emotionally close but live in different cities, provinces or countries.

Today, many fathers want to be more active as parents. Many families have both parents in the paid work force, and many young children get a significant amount of care from people other than their parents. Yet, in this new and complicated world, our role as parents is more important than ever.

What we know about parenting children has also changed, giving us new ways and choices for raising our children. We now know, for instance, that picking up a crying baby will not "spoil" a child. In fact, picking up a crying baby will make her feel more secure.

And we now know that it is better for children if we help them learn how to behave instead of forcing them to obey. Children, in other words, can learn to behave responsibly without fear and punishment.

No matter what your family's make-up or culture, where you were born, or where you live now, as a parent, you are nurturing our world's future citizens. What could be more important?

Babies are born, parents are created

Most of what we have learned about parenting, we have learned from our parents and grandparents. The parent you are is influenced by how you were parented as a child. For some, this was a great experience, for others, not. Either way, these early experiences shaped who you are today.

You can, of course, choose to be—and learn to be—a different parent. You can keep the things you learned that made you feel valued as a person, and throw out those things that didn't. How you parent your child influences who he will be as an adult. Every child needs positive and supportive surroundings to become a healthy, caring, confident adult—and a healthy parent herself one day.

There are as many "right" ways to be a parent as there are parents. What works for one child, may not work for another child, in your family or in someone else's family. Consider what's right for you and your child, but for your child's sake, always make sure your choices are supported by warm, nurturing care (see A *dozen ways to care* below).

Some mothers and fathers appear to easily slip into their roles as parents, others have to work much harder at it. Each parent brings his or her own blend of skills, attitudes, experiences, values and culture to the parenting role. Parents come from different families and can have differing views and approaches. Discussing and understanding each other's experiences will help you bring all these qualities together, to form your own vision for your new family.

Parents are not born—they are created through learning and practice. Committed parents are constantly learning about the skills it takes to create a safe and caring place for their children.

Watch and protect

As a parent, the most powerful thing you can do is give your child loving and supportive care. Nothing gives your child more confidence and security than knowing you are watching and protecting him.

Being a parent is more than just "raising" a child. It is the art and process of helping a baby who is completely dependent on you gain independence during childhood and youth. It's about protecting, nurturing and guiding him when he is young so he learns how to think and make his own good choices as he gets older.

What you can do: A dozen ways to care

You can give your child warm, nurturing care by:

- Letting him know you love him, no matter what.
- Understanding his developmental needs and abilities.
- Protecting him until he can protect himself.
- Helping him learn about the world and people around him.

- Giving him experience suited to his development and personality.
- Playing, singing, talking, reading, learning and having fun together.
- Setting limits for him until he can set his own.
- Responding to him calmly and consistently.
- Being patient—it takes time and repetition for a child to learn.
- Learning new skills to be the best parent you can be.
- Promoting a safe, supportive community for all children.
- Looking after you; your health and well-being are important too.

Forget perfection—aim for your best

Don't worry about being perfect. Nobody is—not you, not your child. You already have the basics of parenting: your love for your child, your instincts and your common sense. When you learn and develop with your child, you will build more skills as you go.

What do you want for your child? How do you want your family to be in 20 years? Will the way you are parenting today get you those results? Asking these questions now is the first step to becoming the parent you want to be.

Be patient and keep trying. Being a great parent doesn't just happen overnight—it's a process.

In writing this book, we've avoided terms such as "good parenting" and "bad parenting." We know you want to be the best parent you can be. At times, that will be easy; at other times, it will be difficult. It's hard to be warm and caring when you're tired, stressed or not feeling well.

When routines get interrupted, when your child is cranky or when someone is telling you what you're doing is wrong, remember that you are the most important influence in your child's life and try your best. Most days, your best is good enough.

You—like every other parent—are only human and will make mistakes. Sometimes you will wish you had done things differently, or that you hadn't done something at all. Look at these times as learning opportunities, not mistakes. Ask yourself what you could have done instead, and what you can do differently next time. Above all, try to show your love everyday and be as consistent as you can. Well known parenting author, Barbara Coloroso explains it like this: "Our children are counting on us to provide two things: consistency and structure. Children need parents who say what they mean, mean what they say, and do what they say they are going to do."

Parenting style

Your personal style is reflected in the clothes you wear, the music you listen to, even the way you talk. Your parenting style can be seen in everything you do in raising your child.

In many parenting resources, three main styles of parenting are described:
- Authoritarian
- Permissive (and/or indifferent)
- Authoritative (or democratic)

In her book, **kids are worth it! Giving Your Child the Gift of Inner Discipline**, parenting consultant Barbara Coloroso describes them as the brickwall, jellyfish and backbone styles.

Authoritarian (brick wall)

Like a **brick wall**, an authoritarian parent imposes a strict and rigid structure, with rules for every aspect of family life. The authoritarian parent makes all family decisions and what the parent thinks is all that matters. They exercise complete control, enforcing it with fear and punishment. Children have little or no participation or choice and tend to be obedient without question (even when it could harm them), fearful or rebellious. Children of this family style are taught "what to think."

Permissive (jellyfish)

Many children raised by authoritarian parents grow up to be **permissive or jellyfish** parents. They know they didn't like how they were raised, and that they don't want to do the same thing with their children, but they may not know what to do instead. Like a jellyfish, structure in this family is shapeless. The parents may be indifferent (don't care what their children do) or permissive (let their children do whatever they want). Jellyfish parents generally have trouble setting limits or rules, and children from these families have difficulty learning respect or responsibility. Children in these families are taught "not to think."

Authoritative (backbone)

Much like a **backbone** that allows the body to be strong, yet able to bend, the authoritative or democratic parent gives a family structure with flexibility. Democratic parents have clear and realistic expectations of their children. Rules are set about things that matter most—safety, responsibility and treating people and property with respect. Limits are clearly defined and kindly, but firmly enforced. Children are taught to respect by being respected. Their opinions and choices are considered. Mistakes are seen as a chance to learn and discipline is used for teaching, not for punishing. Children in these families are taught "how to think."

Some parents swing back and forth between being too permissive and too strict. This is the worst situation for children because it is so unpredictable. Children never know what to expect, and are always anxious and on guard.

The consistency, fairness and respect of the authoritative or democratic parenting style are the elements most likely to create a home in which children can thrive.

What you can do: knowing your parenting style

- What's your style? You may find you are closer to one style or another, especially when you are stressed.
- Are there things you would like to change about your parenting style?
- What is your partner's parenting style? How can you both become more consistent?
- Read on! Growing Miracles can help.
- Learn more; parenting programs are for everyone. Call 211 or Health Link Alberta for information on programs in your community.

Shared parenting

In many families, a couple shares parenting. In these busy times, it can be easy to forget to work on your own relationship as well. Having a strong relationship with your partner helps you be a better parent, and show your child what relationships can be.

Whether you have been together for a long time, or starting a new partnership, it takes time and work to build a good relationship. It helps to remember:

- Good communication is important whether parents are living together or apart. Yelling and fighting are very harmful to children. In a healthy relationship, both partners should feel safe and strong enough to tell each other how they really feel. In a healthy relationship, there is trust and there is no violence. Value and listen to each other even when you do not agree. Work together to find solutions to your problems.

- Parenthood is an emotional journey, especially with the arrival of each child. New parents often have to deal with hormones, a lack of sleep, changing roles and strong or overwhelming feelings. Talking about these things helps. Don't be afraid to express your fears and frustrations. Expect to make mistakes; use them as learning experiences. Give yourselves time to become parents.

- Care for each other. It can be difficult for couples to find private and intimate time, but your relationship is the glue that holds your family together. Spending time together will nurture and strengthen both your relationship and your parenting. Ask family and friends for help so you can have time off from parenting to be alone or to be a couple.

- Find a balance between work and family. Parenthood presents a whole set of questions about family responsibilities, finances and career choices. Will both parents need to have paid work? How long can one parent stay at home? Is it possible for each partner to take time off work? How will you share family responsibilities if you both work away from home? Who will stay home when your child is sick? Talking about your options ahead of time can reduce the stress of parenting.

- Appreciate your differences. A couple is made up of two different people who may share views and attitudes, but may not always do things the same way. Learn about parenting together and talk about what you are feeling and thinking. Even though you may have different styles, what's important is to agree on the overall expectations you have for your child and to be consistent, as much as possible, so your child will know what to expect.

If you are worried about your relationship with your partner, you can find help in many places. Talk to family, friends or someone you trust. For professional support help is just a phone call away. Call the Family Violence Information Line at 310-1818. Trained counsellors are available 24 hours a day, seven days a week and services are offered in more than 170 languages.

If you are sharing your parenting with extended family members, communication and relationship building are just as important. Be sure you are all clear about who is responsible for what.

Balancing life as a parent

Stress is usually an emotional reaction to something that's happening (or happened) in your life. Having a child can be as stressful as it is joyous. While stress is a normal part of life and of being a parent, too much stress can harm you, your child and your family.

If you're more tired, restless, anxious, irritable, confused or emotional than usual, you could be stressed. If stress begins to take over your life, you can manage in many ways. One is to take care of your own needs. As a parent, you may spend much of your time looking after your child. You also need to find time for yourself and for your own interests. It is a balancing act.

Here are a few simple ways to help get stress under control:

- **Take a break.** Soak in the tub for 20 minutes or go for a walk in the park. Let other family members know that everyone needs a little time alone, and that includes you.
- **Make a date.** When parents juggle work or home commitments, appointments, lessons and meals, things can quickly spin out of control. If you feel you have no time, try setting aside an hour, an afternoon or an evening for you (or you and your partner). Don't break the date. It may take a bit of effort to arrange, but it is worth it. Start small; even going out for tea or coffee can be a welcome break.
- **Eat healthy.** Choose foods from all four food groups every day. Try to eat less fat and more whole grains, vegetables and fruit. Eat regular meals and snacks. Limit caffeine, alcohol, sugar and salt. Drink plenty of water (six to eight glasses a day). If you are not able to buy the food you need for your family, your public health nurse can refer you to agencies that can help.
- **Exercise.** Burn off stress with a few minutes of exercise every day. Put your infant in a stroller and take her along for the ride or leave her with her grandparent or a caregiver to enjoy some time alone.
- **Share it.** Parenting is a complex job that can be much easier when you talk to other parents about it. For ideas on meeting other parents, see *Connecting with others* on page 117.
- **Laugh.** It can quickly ease tension and frustration, and improve your mood.
- **Relax.** Use relaxation or meditation techniques; sign up for a yoga class; or play calming music.
- **Get help.** If you are feeling overwhelmed, get professional help. Talk to you doctor or call Health Link Alberta for information on parenting support and/or counselling.

When parents part

Divorce and separation change a family's make-up, but not parents' responsibilities and feelings for their children. Good communication becomes even more important when parenting is divided between two families and two homes.

When parents separate or divorce, it can be as stressful as a death in the family—and it can release a flood of intense emotions. The following advice can help you, your child and your former partner:

First steps

- Tell your child often that both parents still love and support her.
- Children sometimes feel guilty about their parents' separation. Tell your child she is not to blame.
- If the separation is final, make sure your child understands she can't change that.
- Keep to your child's and your family's routine as much as possible.
- Assure your child that both parents are still a part of her life.
- Help your child deal with her feelings by talking about them. Read children's books about separation and divorce with her. Anger, guilt, sadness and confusion are to be expected. If you are concerned about your child's behaviour, ask for help from other family members or a counsellor.

Next steps

- Speak positively about your partner to your child, extended family and friends. If you need to share negative feelings with someone, confide in a trusted and supportive friend or counsellor.
- Support and encourage your child's visits with the other parent. A child is not disloyal to one parent because she likes being with or has fun with the other parent.
- Be cooperative, prompt and friendly to your former partner when your child is picked up or dropped off.
- Let your child talk to the other parent on the phone in between visits.
- Support your child, and respect reasonable limits set by the other parent.
- Don't use your child to find out about your former partner's activities, friends or income.
- To avoid disappointment, arrange visits with the other parent before discussing these plans with your child.
- Keep your child from hearing or seeing disagreements between you and your former partner.

Divorce and separation have a huge effect on children of all ages. Your child will need you and your former partner to work together to continue to parent effectively. If you and your former partner always fight, get help. This behaviour can have a serious and lasting effect on your child.

Local libraries, health centres and support groups offer a wide range of resources for families going through divorce or separation. If you and your family are having a difficult time, call 211 or Health Link Alberta to learn about agencies that provide marriage or divorce counselling.

Parenthood

Miracles
IN PROGRESS

Growing with your child

Your child reaches many milestones in his first six years of life. You'll be thrilled when your baby takes his first steps and says his first words. You may be less excited when he says, "No!" or has his first tantrum. Yet, these are also important milestones that let you know your little miracle is progressing just as he should.

This chapter is an overview of how children grow and what they need from their parents and others who care for them, to stay safe and healthy. The chapters that follow give you more detail about your child's specific age and stage.

Growth and development

Growth is the physical (and visible) change in your child's size and weight. *Development* is the change in your child's physical and mental skills and abilities. Development effects what children can do, how they learn and think, how they react to their emotions and get along with others. Development's gradual changes are more subtle than growth and not always as easy to see.

Growth and development are closely linked. For example, a child's leg muscles and bones must grow and her brain must develop to a certain stage before she is able to walk.

Your child's growth and development depends both on nature (what she is born with) and nurture (what she experiences). Nature, or heredity, plays a role in your child's development, but nurture (your child's surroundings, nutrition and your loving care) is critical for her to reach her full potential.

Patterns of development

While each child grows and develops at his own pace, development follows an orderly pattern: it starts with the head, moves down the body, and then out to the hands and feet. Each stage builds on the one before.

Infants must be able to control their head and neck before they are able to sit. They must sit before they're able to crawl and they crawl before they're able to walk. Babies must babble before they speak and they must feel safe and secure before they trust.

Developmental milestones are markers that tell you your child is developing as expected. These milestones are linked to certain age ranges. While parents may think their children should be able to do things (such as walking and talking) at a specific age, it is normal for children to reach milestones anywhere along the stated range. The descriptions in the charts at the end of this chapter are meant to be guidelines, not hard-and-fast rules. Your child will reach each milestone at his own pace. Don't be surprised if he cuts a tooth at 4 months and don't worry if he is still toothless at 10 months.

You can't change the pace of your child's growth and development, but you can help both in countless ways. *Growing Miracles* outlines many of them.

Along with developmental milestones, each age or stage has *developmental tasks* or things that children must be able to do or learn for healthy development. For example, infants are in the *being* stage. In this stage, their body systems become more stable and they become more aware of their surroundings. As babies start to explore, they move into the *doing* stage. Progressive brain development in the toddler and preschool years create the *thinking* stage, followed by the stage of *identity and power* as new schoolers start to build friendships and learn more about themselves.

By helping your child achieve these developmental tasks in the early years, you create a sense of trust, security and capability. This helps your child form healthy relationships with others, now and throughout his life.

All children have periods of *disequilibrium* as they grow and develop. Disequilibrium is a term used to describe the *off-balance* times that happen just before a child enters a new developmental phase. It is an *out-of-sorts* phase that can occur just before learning something new. Your baby may be cranky as he learns to crawl. As a toddler, he may get pushy as he learns to be around other children and as a preschooler, he may be easily frustrated as he adapts to preschool.

Disequilibrium often triggers an off-balance time for parents, too. Just when you think you have your child figured out, he can change and you have no idea what to do. As frustrating as this is, disequilibrium can be good for both of you as you learn new skills to deal with a new phase. Growing up is tough work, for parents and children alike.

Some parents become frustrated or disappointed by their children's temporary setbacks and may even think their children are lapsing or slipping back on purpose. Whatever your child's age, he's no more able to control this setback or regression than he can control his hunger.

Two steps forward, one step back—it's a natural part of growing and developing. By understanding and supporting your child, you can help him through these phases.

What you can do: give your child time

If your child doesn't do all the things discussed at the various ages, it is hard not to worry. Give him a bit of time.
- Remember, most developmental milestones have an age range.
- Your child may be anywhere along that range and that is perfectly normal. Be patient.

While a small relapse is usually normal, if your child does not recover and move forward or if he completely loses skills already achieved (for example, he stops connecting with you, or stops speaking after he has learned to talk), it could be a signal of a health or developmental problem. You know your child best. If you are concerned or just don't feel right about your child's growth and development, talk to your doctor or public health nurse, or call Health Link Alberta for advice.

Children with disabilities or special needs may not reach all the same milestones at the ages we've outlined. In some cases, they may never reach certain milestones and yet have little difficulty reaching others. Each child should progress according to his own abilities, and each step is cause for celebration.

If your child has a disability, talk to your doctor about what to expect and watch for progress. In Alberta, parents of children with special needs can get support through the Child Disability Resource Link. Call 1-866-346-4661 (toll-free).

Your child's body

Children's bodies and brains grow rapidly in the early years—to reach their potential, they need a balance of good food, sleep, activity and loving care. The healthy habits you teach your child in the early years give her the best chance of a lifetime of wellness.

Brain gain

At birth, a baby's brain is about one-quarter the size of an adult's and is made up of millions of brain cells (called neurons). Brain cells need to connect with each other so a baby can grow and learn, and eventually think—a process that takes many years. These brain cell connections are created through a baby's everyday experiences with her parents and the adults who care for her, and by things and events that she sees, hears, touches, tastes and smells. The more frequent the experience, the stronger the connection.

A baby's brain structure and the earliest brain cell connections are affected by her genes or heredity, and her care during pregnancy. Normally, a baby's senses all work at birth. Your baby is born ready to learn.

As the brain cells connect, pathways are formed to let the many parts of the brain communicate with each other. Over time, connections that are seldom used are shut down. This natural process—called *synaptic pruning*—helps the remaining brain connections work more quickly and effectively. This process of some connections getting stronger and others dissolving continues well into early adulthood. The most critical time for brain development, however, is the early years, as this is when the foundations for all future learning and coping are set.

Brain development takes time; recognizing this will help you better understand your child. When you gaze at your baby and gently talk to her, when you help your toddler learn about her emotions and when you teach your preschooler to solve problems, you are helping build her brain, one step at a time. You can't change the speed, but you are an essential ingredient in your child's development as you learn and grow together. Follow your child's progress through the following chapters and discover the many ways you can help.

As a parent, understanding your child and providing loving care are two of the most important things you can do. Have patience—your child is learning as she grows.

Your brain

Sometimes parenting can feel like a brain drain, but in reality, the arrival of a child triggers some impressive brain activity in moms and dads. Instinctively, parents find they want to watch their baby's every move. This is the first step in learning their baby's cues and how to effectively respond.

From children to seniors, most people want to nurture and protect babies. The urge to hold, touch, rock, comfort, sing to and talk to your baby is your brain's way of letting you know what to do to meet your child's needs.

If you experience depression or a mental illness when your child is born, it may take time to develop these feelings toward your baby. Your illness may also make it hard to cope with the demands of caring for your new baby. Talk with your doctor or public health nurse. Help is available. This book includes many specific examples and tips on coping with the stress of parenting and where to find help if you're concerned about your mental health.

Brain food

To develop properly, the brain needs nourishment and activity.

Breastmilk is the ideal *brain food*. For the first six months of your child's life it provides all the nutrition he needs. The longer you breastfeed, the greater the benefits to you and your child. Breastfeeding is recommended until your child is 2 years or older.

Nutritious food is very important for proper brain development. *Canada's Food Guide* is the basis for healthy eating throughout your child's life. *Growing Miracles* outlines the roles that both you and your child have in a healthy eating relationship, and helps you understand the various stages and phases of eating throughout early childhood.

Your baby also needs experiences to help his brain grow. Nothing activates an infant's brain better than another person, especially a parent or loved one. Talking, playing, reading, singing, touching and comforting are all activities that nourish a growing brain. Vibrant mobiles, cuddly teddy bears and lively DVD programs may seem interesting, but your baby prefers your voice, face and touch above anything else. Enjoy the attention and know you're the best teacher and toy your young child could ever have.

Like all growth and development in your child, the brain can't be rushed—at any age. You can't make your child smarter by reading him university textbooks. What you can do is love, nurture and encourage him to learn and explore at his own pace, in his own way.

Eating

Eating is essential to life. How and what your child eats and drinks is important to her growth and development. Good nutrition is a key element in building the foundation for a lifetime of good health, but it is more than just eating.

During the early years, you and your child can develop a healthy feeding relationship: you decide *where* and *what* your child eats and she decides *if* she eats and *how* much. *When* you feed your child will depend on your child's age. Your infant needs to be fed when she is hungry. You will quickly recognize when she is telling you she is hungry or full.

Once she is well established on solid food, *when* you feed your child will be more your responsibility. Children do best when they eat three meals and three planned snacks a day, based on Canada's Food Guide. Knowing how to choose and serve healthy food will benefit your whole family.

Mealtime is a wonderful chance for families to take time out of their busy days to connect. Research shows that when families eat dinner together four or more times a week, children eat better, they are less likely to have eating problems, they get along better with others, and they do better in school. The time you spend in sharing a meal builds strong family bonds. Eat together. Talk together. Make meals and memories together.

Healthy teeth

The best way to help your child develop healthy dental practices is to set a good example. Help her by:
- Limiting snacks high in sugar
- Cleaning her teeth at least twice a day
- Supervising her brushing and flossing until she is at least 8 years old
- Visiting a dentist regularly

Teeth and fluoride

Fluoridated tap water is strictly regulated and provides extra protection against tooth decay. Fluoridated toothpaste also reduces the risk of cavities, but it has 1,500 times more fluoride than fluoridated water. Because children end up swallowing toothpaste if they are unable to spit, children under 3 years should not use fluoridated toothpaste, unless your dentist recommends otherwise. Once your child starts using toothpaste, teach her to rinse and spit out after brushing her teeth. No one should swallow toothpaste.

Sleeping

Sleep lets the body rest and grow. It restores our bodies and minds. While we sleep, our bodies heal and repair; our brains organize and store thoughts and memories. When children sleep, their bodies produce a growth hormone and chemicals important to the immune system. Good sleep habits are essential to your child's growth, development and health

Children need different amounts of sleep at different ages. *Growing Miracles* can help you understand your child's sleep needs at each stage and give you ideas for building good sleep habits that benefit your child for life.

Activity

Physical activity is important for proper growth and fortunately, children have a built-in desire to be active. It is called play! Children need to play as much as they need to eat and sleep. Play has many different purposes and your child needs your help to balance the many kinds of play.

Free unstructured play is important for children's brain development. Children need active play with freedom and space to develop their skills, burn off energy and gain a love for active, healthy living. Without this type of play, children face the risk of developmental delays, obesity and other health effects of an inactive lifestyle.

More structured activities led by parents are important too. Whether it is a family bike ride or an evening soccer game in the local park, when you participate, you are a role model and your children are much more likely to learn and adopt good attitudes towards activity. Children learn about activity by watching it and doing it. Keep the focus on participation and fun. Having a positive attitude towards physical activity is good for both you and your child.

Infants, babies and toddlers need an adult's close, active supervision whenever they are awake and especially when they are active. Stay close by so you can keep your child safe and help if needed. As your child gets older, your supervision can gradually move further away but your child always needs to know that he can come to you for help.

Your child's mind

Children are born ready to learn. Like a sponge, their brains soak up everything around them. How and when they learn is closely linked to their individual growth and development. Just as every child grows and develops at his own pace, he also learns at his own pace.

Three important elements are related to learning in young children: speech, language and play.

Children learn speech and language through their contact with others. Speech and language development, like other development, follows fairly predictable stages.

Your baby's *coos* and *goos* will become babbling and sounds, followed by his first words and, as understanding increases, gradually longer sentences and conversations. Your child should be able to talk by the age of 2 and be understood by the age of 3. What begins as simple sounds becomes thousands of words by the time your child is an adult.

Children are born with the ability to learn speech and language, but must have help. They need people to talk to them, to help them understand what is said and to let them practise the language, or languages, around them. Children have the ability to learn any language. The languages your child learns (whether it is English, Cantonese, Vietnamese or Punjabi) depends on what he experiences.

Language helps us understand our world. We use language skills to learn, express ourselves and build relationships. They are the foundations of literacy (the ability to read and write) and lifelong learning. Communication skills grow quickly during the first six years of life. Children need as many chances as possible to hear and use language during this time. It's never too soon to start reading to your child. Read every day. It is a fun way for children to experience language right from the start!

Play is often thought of as fun and carefree, which is exactly what it should be. It is also much, much more—play is one of the main ways your child learns. Because free play is unstructured and without formal rules, it taps into a child's imagination. Through free play, children learn to be creative, to discover things about themselves and their world, and learn social skills and problem solving.

At first, your child learns to play by interacting with you. Watch what interests her, make sure her environment is safe, and then let her explore her new world. As your child grows, she needs to have the chance to play with other children too. This is how she learns who she is and how people get along.

Active play and the development of physical skills are very important in the first six years of your child's life. The simple movements learned during his early years are the foundation for all the complex and coordinated movements he'll learn in the future. The more your child plays, the more he learns, physically and mentally.

New words build language and new movements build skills - and play is a great way to learn both. Speech, language and play can be combined in many wonderful ways to help your child learn. You will find many suggestions and examples for encouraging language and play throughout the book.

Emotional development

Emotional development is the process of learning about, and coping with, emotions and feelings. The early years are a critical time for your child's emotional development. With your help, your child can:

- Learn about her feelings and how to control and express them in healthy ways
- Learn to care about others
- Develop a healthy self-esteem (feeling of self-worth).

As parents, we spend lots of time teaching our children tasks such as tying their shoes or putting away their toys. We need to give them just as much help in learning how to handle their feelings such as anger, sadness or frustration. From the very first time children wrinkle their brows, smile at a parent's face, or test the limits of their lungs with a hearty cry, it's obvious that emotions are a main part of being human. Feelings come naturally to all of us, and learning to deal with them is one of life's most important lessons.

Babies depend on their parents to help them focus and learn how to deal with overwhelming feelings. When you are able to respond to your child's cues in a sensitive way and help her celebrate her joy and decrease her distress, you are building the basic brain connections that build emotional regulation. When you help your child do this at a young age, it is easier for her to learn to do it on her own as she gets older.

As a parent, you have the greatest influence on this part of your child's development.

Attachment

Attachment is the sense of security your child gains from knowing you (his parents) are willing and able to offer comfort and safety. Attachment gets stronger every time you respond to your child's cues, watch over and delight in his explorations, and comfort him when he needs you (especially when he is sick, hurt or emotionally upset). Your child's sense of security continues to develop with your loving care as he grows.

Attachment is important to your child's emotional and social development. When his needs are met, he learns to trust and feels secure and valued. When your child has a secure attachment with you, he can then learn to trust and get along with others. He will be more confident as he grows and less likely to have social or emotional problems as he gets older.

Your child's world

During the early years, children develop a sense of who they are and how they can get along with others. Emotional development and social development are closely connected. Healthy development in both these areas shapes the adult a child becomes.

Social development is the process of learning how to act around and get along with others. As your child develops socially, she will learn first to discover things, then to explore and finally to play. For example, when an infant discovers her feet, they soon become her favourite playthings. As a young toddler, she discovers she is a separate being and that other children may look just like her. She explores these other children, but is not yet interested in playing with them. She will, however, like to watch them and play beside them. Eventually she learns to play with other children, learns to share and learns to get along with others. This process takes place gradually throughout the early years.

Children who have healthy emotional and social development are able to form empathy (the ability to understand how another person feels), a quality needed to get along with and care about others.

Childcare choices

The decision to leave your child in someone else's care can be very emotional. Childcare can create anxiety for both parents and children of any age. While cost and location will be a concern, the most important thing to look for is quality care. Knowing your child is safe and well cared for will greatly reduce your anxiety when you must be apart.

Quality childcare

Whether you are choosing a daycare centre, a family day home or a relative to care for your child, take the time to make sure the care she gets while you are away is top quality. Give yourself lots of time to explore your options. Feeling comfortable with your child's caregivers makes it easier to work together as a team.

When you are considering a daycare or family day home for your child, the Canadian Child Care Federation recommends you look for childcare providers that:
- Understand how children grow and learn
- Are affectionate and responsive to children's needs
- Know how to provide safe and healthy care for children
- Provide a stable environment with activities that encourage learning and play
- Work together with you as a team
- Know about resources and programs in the community
- Use appropriate strategies for guiding behaviour.

What to look for

The daycare or day home you are considering should:
- Be clean, safe and secure
- Have a warm and caring atmosphere
- Have the best interests of your child as their main goal
- Have books, toys and activities for different ages
- Have child-adult ratios that are appropriate to the type of care they provide
- Provide a variety of play spaces (indoor, outdoor, active and quiet)
- Follow a flexible, yet predictable routine
- Provide healthy meals and snacks
- Be inclusive and respectful of different languages and cultures
- Have established policies about child guidance.

What you can do: starting childcare

Once you find childcare you are comfortable with, you can focus on adjusting to new routines. The following can help:

- Spend time at the daycare centre or day home with your child. Be there as your child explores her new surroundings and begins to build trust with the caregiver(s).

- Do a couple of trial runs by leaving your child for short periods with her new caregiver(s) before starting full time.

- Have your child take something familiar to childcare. Some children bring a favourite blanket, stuffed animal or family picture.

- When you leave your child, talk to her about what is going to happen. Leaving without telling her can damage the trust you've built with her. Tell her that you are leaving, where you are going and that you will come back and pick her up at the end of your day. Help her express feelings such as fear or sadness. It's normal for children to be upset when their parents leave. Say goodbye in a loving, calm manner and leave.

- When you return to pick her up, comment to your child on how you have come back as you said that you would. This will help her to understand that you will always come back to get her and will increase her sense of trust and security in her new routine. In the early years, your child is just learning object permanence (that things can go away and come back again).

- If you act secure (even if you may not feel it), it will help your child feel secure and know that she will be okay. Your child will begin to understand that this is a new part of her routine and that she is safe.

- If your child has special needs, make sure a childcare provider is able to meet them. Children with special needs in high-quality, inclusive childcare do just as well or better than those in segregated settings.

Protecting your child

Young children are completely dependent on their parents or guardians to protect and guide them until they are able to cope on their own. You can do many things to help your child be as healthy and safe as possible.

Preventing injuries

Children must have safe environments to develop healthy bodies and minds. If they can't explore safely, their creativity and learning suffer and they face a greater risk of injury, as they don't have the physical or mental skills to protect themselves. Remember, though, that your child needs to be active. A safe environment protects your child from injury without limiting her ability to be physically active.

Injuries are the leading cause of death and disability for children in Alberta. More children die each year from injuries than from all childhood diseases combined. Yet, most injuries are predictable and preventable—they are not accidents.

Most childhood injuries occur at home. When you know the risks (and take steps to reduce them), you can prevent the most common causes: falls, choking, poisoning and scalds, as well as injuries during outdoor play and travel. Risks to young children's safety include:

- **Falls.** The risk of falling changes as children grow and develop. When they are wriggling and kicking as babies, they can fall off furniture. Once they start to move, they can also fall out of baby equipment, down stairs and out of windows. As they grow taller and can reach higher, they climb and can pull things over on themselves. As their play moves outdoors, falls from bikes and playground equipment increase.
- **Choking and poisoning.** Young children explore by putting things in their mouths, so choking and poisoning are very real dangers. Childproof your home and keep small objects and poisonous substances away from your child.
- **Scalds and burns.** The most common burns in young children are scalds caused by hot liquids and foods. You can avoid scalds by making sure your tap water is no higher than 49 °C (120 °F), usually the warm setting on your hot water heater. To test your water's temperature, run the hot water tap for two minutes and then fill a cup. Use a meat or candy thermometer to test. Once you have adjusted the temperature of your hot water heater, retest the temperature in 24 hours. As well, keep hot foods and drinks away from young children and make sure your child is safely out of the way when you are cooking.
- **Lack of supervision.** As a parent, you need to be constantly alert and paying attention to your young child. Understanding typical development for your child's age can help you anticipate situations

in which they can be hurt. Make sure to check safety devices often for signs of wear. While you may use many of the safety devices available (for example, safety straps on strollers and childproof cupboard latches), never rely on safety devices to completely protect your child. Your supervision remains the most important thing in keeping your child safe.

Vehicle travel

Many children travel in a vehicle every day—to childcare, playschool or out with their moms or dads. Travelling in a vehicle poses risks for everyone, but particularly for children because of their small size. No one plans on collisions; they can happen when they are least expected.

When your vehicle comes to an abrupt stop (like it does in a crash), anything not restrained in the vehicle—a child, a toy or a bag of groceries—continues to move at the same speed as when the vehicle was moving. A crash does not necessarily have to be serious to cause serious injuries to infants and children. Young passengers can be seriously hurt when a car stops or swerves suddenly.

When used properly, car seats—from rear-facing infant seats to booster seats—save lives. Children are too small to fit into adult-sized seat belts. Young children need to ride in a properly installed car seat, appropriate for their age and size, every time they get into a vehicle. Not only is it the law, it's good common sense.

Using a child safety seat properly can reduce the likelihood of your child being injured or killed in a crash by as much as 75 per cent. Infants and children rely on their parents and caregivers to make every ride a safe ride, and you can do it. Carefully follow the car seat manufacturer's instructions and read your vehicle owner's manual when putting in any car seat. Ask your public health nurse or Health Link Alberta for a copy of the Yes Test for the type of car seat you are using. When you have completed the checklist, you can be confident you have installed your car seat properly. You may be fined if your car seat is used or installed incorrectly.

The safest place for your child's car seat is in the back seat of your vehicle. Never put a car seat in front of an airbag. The force of an airbag inflating, even in a minor crash, has been known to kill young children. In fact, children under 12 should not ride in the front seat of any vehicle equipped with airbags. Make it a household rule and enjoy the fact that no one argues over who gets the front seat—at least for a few years.

For more information on car seats or free car seat education classes in your community, contact Health Link Alberta.

Second-hand smoke

Second-hand smoke is the smoke blown into the air by a smoker and the smoke that comes from the end of a burning cigarette, cigar or pipe. It contains more than 4,000 chemicals, many of them known to cause cancer. Second-hand smoke is bad for everyone and is especially harmful to children because their lungs are smaller and they breathe faster than adults.

Opening a window, smoking in another room, air purifiers or ventilation systems are not enough to protect you or your child from the harmful effects of second-hand smoke.

Exposure to second-hand smoke is a major risk factor of SIDS (sudden infant death syndrome). Children exposed to second-hand smoke are more likely to develop health problems such as ear infections, croup, bronchitis, pneumonia and long-term breathing conditions such as asthma. They are also at greater risk of developing leukemia and other forms of cancer.

If you're a smoker, the best thing you can do for you and your child is quit. If you cannot quit, smoke outside, away from open windows and air intake vents. Where you smoke matters. Smoke residue lasts a long time on your hair and clothing and in enclosed spaces, and remains harmful even after you finish smoking. Do not smoke in your car, even if your child is not with you.

A clean home is . . .

. . . a healthier home. Your home needn't be and shouldn't be sterile, but cleanliness is important for your child's good health. Diapering areas, bedding, clothing, toys, bathrooms and floors (where older babies and toddlers can spend so much time) need to be cleaned regularly.

No house is dust free, but if your baby is exposed to too much dust, it could contribute to the development of asthma and allergies.

Dust on floors and carpets can contain dust mites, moulds, pet dander and chemicals. When babies and small children crawl or play on floors, they pick up dust on their hands. Their hands usually end up in their mouths.

To keep your baby from eating dust and other contaminants off the floor, keep your floors clean, and wash your baby's hands after he has been crawling on the floor. Put your baby on a clean blanket on the floor for his daily *tummy time* (see *Encourage movement* page 68). Dust your baby's room often using a clean, damp cloth.

Food safety

Children's small body size makes them more likely to get sick from food that is not stored, prepared or cooked properly. To protect your child's health, take care in storing, preparing, and cooking food.

Storing food

- Refrigerate perishable food as soon as possible after buying or preparing. Store leftovers in clean containers.
- Keep your refrigerator below 4 °C (40 °F) and your freezer at -18 °C (0 °F).

Preparing food

- Wash your hands before handling any food, and after handling food such as raw meat, poultry and fish.
- Wash fresh fruit and vegetables before cutting or serving.
- Avoid touching other food while you are preparing raw meat, poultry or fish unless you have washed your hands.
- Clean all kitchen surfaces, utensils and equipment after using.
- Change and wash kitchen towels often to prevent germs from spreading.
- Any surface that comes in contact with raw meat, poultry or fish can be sanitized, after washing, with a solution of 2 ml (¹/₂ tsp.) of household bleach in one litre of water. Change your dishcloth and wash your hands.

Cooking

- Cook all meats, poultry, fish and eggs to safe temperatures, using a food thermometer.
- Use glass or microwave-safe containers only when using the microwave to prevent chemicals from leaching into your child's food.
- Reheat leftovers to 74 °C (165 °F).

Foods to avoid

Avoid certain foods when feeding children.

- For children under 1 year old, avoid:
  - Honey (may contain bacteria that causes infant botulism)
  - Any liquids from a propped bottle.
- Until children are 4 years old, avoid foods that can cause choking such as:
  - Popcorn, nuts or seeds
  - Fish with bones

- Whole hot dogs or sausages (if serving, cut into long strips, then into bite-sized pieces)
- Fruit with pits (cherries, plums or peaches are okay to serve if skinned, pitted and cut up)
- Raw, hard vegetables (cut into narrow strips or grate)
- Snacks with toothpicks or skewers
- Hard, round or smooth foods such as candies, cough drops, gum, raisins and whole grapes
- Spoonfuls of foods that can stick to the roof of the mouth (for example, peanut butter or cream cheese).

For all children of all ages:
- Avoid foods with little or no nutritional value, such as:
  - Chocolate
  - Potato chips
  - Soft drinks, drink crystals and sport drinks
  - Tea, coffee and herbal teas
  - Salt and pickles
  - Foods with sugar substitutes
  - Low-fat or calorie-reduced foods.
- Avoid foods that can make anyone sick, and are particularly harmful to young children:
  - Raw sprouts (alfalfa, radish or bean); cooked sprouts are safe to eat
  - Any food containing raw eggs (such as cookie dough or Caesar salad dressing made with raw eggs)
  - Unpasteurized fruit juice, milk or cheese
  - Undercooked meats, poultry, fish or eggs
  - Food that has not been stored properly.
- Although fish is an excellent source of protein and healthy fats, some fish may have high levels of mercury. This is of concern as it can harm a developing brain and nervous system. Pregnant and breastfeeding women, infants and young children should avoid the higher risk choices. For the most current information, visit Health Canada's site at: www.healthcanada.gc.ca (search "mercury and fish questions").

If you have a family history of food or other allergies, talk to your doctor for specific recommendations about your child's diet.

For general questions about feeding young children, ask your public health nurse for a copy of *Feeding Baby Solid Foods* and/or *Healthy Eating and Active Living for Your One to Five Year Old*, or contact Health Link Alberta.

The great outdoors

Being outside is good for children. While outside, however, children need protection from the sun, insects, heat and cold. Just one sunburn can increase your child's risk of skin cancer later in life. Insect bites are irritating and can cause disease. Children's small bodies are at greater risk of becoming too hot or too cold, putting them at risk of heat stroke or hypothermia. When your child is going outdoors, winter or summer, keep these things in mind:

- **Babies under 1 year**
  Health Canada recommends that all children under 1 year be kept out of direct sunlight. Very little research has been done on the long-term effects of using sunscreen or insect repellent on babies. It is best to protect babies' delicate skin by using clothing, shade and mosquito netting. See directions below on when to use sunscreen and insect repellent.

- **Children over 1 year**
  As your child grows, teach her to play in the shade. Look for shady play spaces at home and in your community. The sun's rays are strongest from 11:00 a.m. to 4:00 p.m.; avoid being in the sun at these times. Loose fitting, light-coloured clothing will keep your child cool and protected. Keep bare arms and legs covered whenever possible. A wide-brimmed hat protects the face and neck. Use sunscreen and insect repellent as directed below.

What you can do: sunscreen and insect repellent

Sunscreen

Protect children from the sun's harmful rays with sunscreen. Choose a sunscreen with a sun protection factor (SPF) of 15 or higher that protects from both UVA and UVB rays:

- For children under 6 months of age, do not use sunscreen. Avoid direct sunlight (see page 78).

- For children 6 months to 1 year, apply sunscreen only if being in the sun is unavoidable. It is best to keep your baby out of the direct sun, but if you have to be in the sun, it is better to use sunscreen than to let your baby's skin burn. Apply 20 minutes before going out in the sun.

- For children 1 year and older, apply 20 minutes before going outside and re-apply every two hours and after wet or sweaty activities.

Insect repellent

Use the least concentrated formula of DEET (10 per cent or less) for children.

Apply to exposed skin and clothing. Avoid your child's face and hands. Do not use on irritated skin. Always use insect repellent sparingly and avoid prolonged use.

- For children under 6 months of age, do not use insect repellent. Use mosquito netting and avoid being out when insect activity is high.
- For children ages 6 months to 2 years, apply only when there is a high risk of complications from insect bites; use once a day only.
- For children 2 years and older, insect repellent can be applied up to three times a day.

Wash it off

When sun and insect protection are no longer needed, wash your child's skin thoroughly with soap and warm water.

All weather protection

Help your child beat the heat by encouraging her to drink water. In winter, keep your child warm by dressing in layers and using warm mitts and boots; don't bundle tightly. Scarves that hang down can catch and strangle your child; neck warmers are a safer choice. If you are using a blanket for warmth, put it over your child after he is buckled safely into his car seat. Hats keep your child cool in the summer and warm in the winter—they are an essential item of clothing for children in Canada.

Keeping your child healthy

Your child's health is precious—protect it by teaching her healthy habits, taking her for regular checkups and getting her vaccinated against childhood diseases.

The following general guidelines are for children of all ages. These guidelines are the basics; more age-specific suggestions are outlined in the chapters to come.

Wash away germs

The key to better health is in your hands. Like health care experts around the world, Alberta Health Services considers handwashing the single most effective way to prevent the spread of disease.

When you wash your hands regularly, you set a good example for your child. Regularly washing your hands and your child's hands reduces the spread of germs. In homes, the most common ways your hands can spread disease-causing germs are:

- Preparing food with unclean hands.
- Not washing your hands after diapering your baby or using the toilet.
- Not washing your hands between preparing raw foods (meat, poultry or fish) and other foods (such as sandwiches and salads).
- Sneezing, blowing your nose or coughing and then touching something or someone before washing your hands.
- Touching raw meat and then putting your hands in your mouth. Children should never be allowed to touch raw meat as they can easily spread germs from their hands to their mouth and can get very sick.

When to wash

Everyone in your home will be healthier when they wash their hands before:

- Preparing food
- Feeding your child (including breastfeeding)
- Eating (at home or away)
- Giving medication to your child
- Cleaning your child's gums or flossing and brushing her teeth.

And after:

- Handling raw meat, poultry or fish
- Coughing, sneezing or blowing your nose or helping a child blow her nose
- Changing diapers (wash your baby's hands too)
- Using the toilet or helping a child use the toilet
- Caring for a sick child or family member
- Cleaning up vomit, bowel movements, urine or other body fluids
- Touching any animals, including pets, or cleaning their litter box, cage or removing their waste from the yard (adults and children)
- Working in the garden or handling pesticides or manure
- Coming back from a public place (for example, the mall, school, work), or coming in from being outside.

What you can do: how to wash hands

1. Use warm running water and plain soap.
2. Rub the insides and backs of both hands and between your fingers until you have many soap bubbles. Do this for 20 seconds to remove germs, such as bacteria and viruses, from your hands.
3. Rinse your hands under warm running water.
4. Dry your hands with a clean towel.

Keeping it clean

- Encourage a life-long handwashing habit by starting early with your new baby. Use a separate, clean cloth and towel just for your baby.
- As your child gets older, make handwashing fun by singing the ABC song—it keeps him washing for the right amount of time and he will learn the alphabet at the same time!
- Antibacterial (antimicrobial) soap is not necessary at home because it kills both the good and bad bacteria on the skin. Good bacteria live on skin and protect against infections. Antibacterial soaps add to the growing problem of antibiotic resistance.
- Change and wash bathroom and kitchen towels often to prevent germs from spreading.
- If there is vomiting or diarrhea in the home, use a disinfectant on bathroom surfaces and fixtures. Wash, then disinfect any soiled surfaces with a solution of 1 part bleach mixed with 50 parts warm water until the illness is over.

Regular checkups

Regular checkups with your doctor, dentist and optometrist are important to your child's good health:

- **Doctor:** Set up a schedule with your doctor or pediatrician. A healthy child should see her doctor regularly in their first year and then at least once a year as she gets older.
- **Dentist:** Your child should see a dentist on or around her first birthday and have a full checkup by the age of 2 to 3. If you cannot afford dental care, contact Alberta Child Health Benefit Plan (see next page). Health Link Alberta can also advise you if alternative services are available in your community.

- **Optometrist:** Your child's first eye examination should be at 6 months old, again at 3 years old and yearly from the age of 5 years. If you are concerned about your child's vision, or think she has an eye infection, don't wait. Contact your optometrist right away so treatment can begin as soon as possible. In Alberta, the provincial government fully pays for eye examinations for children 18 years old and under. No referral is needed to visit an optometrist, so parents can book appointments directly.

Alberta Child Health Benefit Plan

If money is a problem for your family, you may be eligible for the Alberta Child Health Benefit Plan. This premium-free health benefit plan provides dental, optical, emergency ambulance, essential diabetic supplies and prescription drug coverage for children in low-income families. For information, call 310-0000 or visit http://employment.alberta.ca/FCH/2076.html

Community Health Centres

Alberta Health Services has community health centres in convenient urban and rural locations around the province. Community health centres are listed in the telephone book and on Alberta Health Services website: www.albertahealthservices.ca

Whether in the city or rural area, each community health centre offers a variety of community health programs and services, including many for parents of young children. Public health nurses are a good source of information and support. They offer help with everything from visiting you in your home when your baby first arrives, to providing vaccination and health counselling at well child clinics.

Vaccination

Whooping cough, tetanus, polio, measles and diphtheria—a few short decades ago, the mere mention of these diseases caused fear and concern. Thanks to vaccinations, these and other diseases are now rare in North America and many other countries around the world.

The United Nations (UN) estimates that immunization has saved more than 20 million lives worldwide in the past two decades. The spread of new infectious diseases, however, underlines the need for continued vaccination. The UN states that:

- Vaccines protect whole communities. Infectious diseases, by definition, spread easily, however, viruses and bacteria can also be stopped in their tracks if enough people are immunized. The more children in a community who are fully immunized against certain diseases, the safer everyone is.
- Diseases can reappear when immunization drops. In Eastern Europe in the 1990s, low immunization rates along with economic crises triggered a major epidemic of diphtheria that killed 30,000 people. The epidemic spread to Finland, Germany and Norway before it was contained.
- Vaccines are effective. With the exception of providing safe drinking water, no other health intervention is as effective as immunization for reducing disease and mortality rates.
- Vaccines are affordable. In Alberta, routine childhood vaccinations are free.

To stay protected, your child needs his vaccinations at the correct times. Some vaccines provide protection for life; others need to be *boosted* after a certain period. If your child has not been vaccinated or has fallen behind on the schedule, it is never too late to catch up. Talk to your public health nurse. For a complete schedule of routine vaccinations, or more information about vaccines and the diseases they prevent, see the Alberta Health Services' prenatal book *From Here Through Maternity*, ask your public health nurse or call Health Link Alberta.

Is my child sick?

Illness can strike any child at any time. Be prepared for illness by knowing the general signs to watch for:

- Unusual behaviour or a change in behaviour
- Runny nose, cough, wheezing or difficulty breathing
- Vomiting
- Diarrhea
- Dehydration (dark coloured urine; dry skin, mouth or tongue)
- Change in skin colour
- Rash
- Fever (see next page).

If your child shows any of these symptoms, monitor his condition carefully and call Health Link Alberta or see your doctor if you're concerned.

For information about the signs of illness in children under the age of 1, see *Is my baby sick?* on page 61.

Taking your child's temperature

You can take your baby's temperature at home by using the armpit method with a digital thermometer (see below). It's the easiest and most accurate way of checking for fever at home in newborns and young children.

The normal body temperature, taken under the arm:

- For babies from birth to 28 days old is 36.5 to 37.3 °C (97.7 to 99.1 °F)
- For children 29 days and older is 34.7 to 37.3 °C (94.5 to 99.1 °F)

A body temperature above 37.3 °C (99.1 °F) is considered a fever.

Using a digital thermometer

A digital thermometer is easier and safer to use than a glass-type with mercury and more accurate than the ear-type available for home use. To safely use a digital thermometer, follow these steps:

1. Clean the thermometer with cool, soapy water and rinse.
2. Loosen your child's clothes to the waist.
3. Place the thermometer horizontally under the arm, so that the tip is in the centre of the armpit and the other end extends out front. Make sure your child's arm is tucked snugly, but gently, against her body.
4. Leave the thermometer in place for about one minute, until you hear the *beep*.
5. Remove the digital thermometer and read the temperature.
6. Clean the thermometer by following the manufacturer's instructions. If instructions are not available, clean the thermometer with warm, soapy water, rinse with cool water and dry before putting away.

For more information or help deciding what to do about a fever, call Health Link Alberta.

Learning more

Parenting is all about helping your child grow and learn, and keeping him safe and healthy. Although *Growing Miracles* focuses on the early years, the learning—and the journey—never really ends. To learn more about being a parent, parenting programs and resources available to you, talk to your public health nurse, call Health Link Alberta or visit www.healthlinkalberta.ca.

HEALTHLink Alberta

Health advice 24 hours a day

Toll-free: 1-866-408-LINK (5465)

Calgary: 403-943-LINK (5465)   Edmonton: 780-408-LINK (5465)

Development: Birth to 3 months | The being stage

Tasks	Milestones
This is the **being stage**, a time when it's important for your child to learn: • Attachment—the emotional bond between you and your child, and how you relate to each other • Trust—knowing that good, dependable and loving care is always there	**Physical** • Kicks and grasps based on reflexes • Has weak neck muscles and heavy head; can turn head by reflex, then begins to gain control of it and turn with purpose • Feeding/sleeping is unpredictable when newborn; more predictable over time • Discovers hands and can bring them to mouth **Cognitive: learning and thinking** • Learns from birth • Is startled by loud noises • Makes pleasure sounds: *coos* and *goos* • Prefers people to toys **Emotional** • Cries to signal needs • Crying increases at 2 weeks; peaks in intensity around 2 months; and gradually decreases by 3 to 4 months • Generally quiets when comforted; may have times when can't stop crying • Depends on parents and others to cope with emotions • Feels safe when needs are met • Begins to learn how to self-soothe **Social** • Smiles to express pleasure by 2 months • Recognizes and prefers familiar faces and voices

Tasks	Milestones
This continues to be the **being stage**, a time when it's important for your child to learn: • Attachment—the emotional bond between you and your child, and how you relate to each other • Trust—knowing that good, dependable and loving care is always there	**Physical** • Reaches for objects • Puts hands together • On tummy, pushes up and lifts head and chest off floor • Gains more head control, holds head steady • Begins to sit with support—balance improves over time • Rolls from tummy to back and then from back to tummy • Swallowing pattern changes to get ready for eating solid foods • Doubles birthweight by 6 months **Cognitive: learning and thinking** • Explores by reaching, grasping and putting things in mouth • Turns head towards sounds • Makes lots of noises—babbles, coos, gurgles • Repeats actions and sounds to get desired response from parents and others • Begins to get excited at sight of food **Emotional** • Has different cries for different needs • Self-soothes more, but still needs comfort from parent • Shows emotions with face, body, voice and actions • Forming attachment to primary caregiver **Social** • Smiles and laughs • Aware of and prefers familiar faces • Enjoys being near people • Responds to people's voices and face expressions

Development: 6 to 12 months | The doing stage

Tasks	Milestones
This is the **doing stage**, a time when it's important for your child to keep learning about earlier tasks as well as: • Discovery—learning about her world through touch, grasp, reach and taste	**Physical** • Sits up with support, then sits by self • Crawls and rolls • Picks up things with finger and thumb • Helps or resists dressing/undressing • Helps or resists feeding • First teeth appear • Has more organized sleep patterns; can settle self back to sleep during night • Usually naps twice during the day • Pulls up to stand and walks holding furniture • Triples birthweight (by 1 year) **Cognitive: learning and thinking** • Babbles a lot; imitates sounds and actions • Starts to recognize words and simple phrases • Gets excited at the sight of food • Realizes things exist even when out of sight (object permanence) • Responds to own name • Points to familiar things • Continues to explore by putting things in mouth • Says a few words, not always clearly • Starts to remember and likes routines • Likes to stack, nest and put things in containers **Emotional** • May show fear or anxiety over people and situations previously accepted • Likes to stay close to parents/primary caregiver • Shows pleasure when parents/primary caregiver return • Seeks comfort when upset • Starts to "read" emotions of others **Social** • Enjoys games such as *Peek-a-Boo* and *Pat-a-Cake* • Anxious around strangers • May cry or cling when parents leave • Plays purposefully with toys

Development: 12 to 18 months | The doing stage

Tasks	Milestones
This is the **doing stage**, a time when it's important for your child to keep learning about earlier tasks as well as: • Autonomy— that he is a separate person from you	**Physical** • Helps feed self: picks up food with fingers, tries to hold spoon and drink from cup • Stands up without assistance • Walks holding your hand or on own • Crawls up and down stairs • Develops food preferences • Tries to throw ball • Builds tower of two to four blocks • Scribbles with crayon • Takes off clothes **Cognitive: learning and thinking** • Knows things exist even when out of sight (object permanence) • Likes to look for dropped or hidden objects • Points finger to ask for something or show interest • Follows simple instructions • Begins pretend-play • Says more words every month • Points to familiar objects or body parts when asked • Favourite words become *no* and *mine* • Likes simple stories, picture books, songs and rhymes **Emotional** • Begins to assert independence • Resists limits • Has favourite toy or blanket for comfort and security • Has mood swings and tantrums **Social** • Develops fear of strange objects and events, and separation from parents • Likes to watch and be with other children • Cannot yet play cooperatively • Imitates others' actions • Starts to show concern for others • Not yet able to share

Miracles

Tasks	Milestones
This is the **thinking stage**, a time when it's important for your child to keep learning about earlier tasks as well as: • Exploration—learning about her world and how it works	**Physical** • Walks up and down stairs with help • Kicks a ball while standing • Runs • Likes riding toys • Climbs on and over furniture • Opens doors • Feeds self, but is messy **Cognitive: learning and thinking** • Points to pictures when named • Can help turn book pages • Completes simple inset puzzles • Understands more words than can say • Begins to use two-word sentences • Enjoys and moves to music • Likes simple games and rhymes (*Itsy Bitsy Spider, Hide and Seek*) **Emotional** • Explores from *secure base* of parent or caregiver • Has tantrums due to frustration, tiredness • Starts recognizing emotions in self and others • Has more fears and anxieties; night terrors peak at age 2 • Shows affection • Gets frustrated when unable to do things • May hit, slap or bite • Finds comfort in routines **Social** • Feels strong ownership; hoards toys • Plays beside but not with children • May try to comfort others • Recognizes self and family in photographs • Finds sharing difficult

Tasks

Milestones

This is the **thinking stage**, a time when it's important for your child to keep learning about earlier tasks as well as:

- Emotions—to be aware of and able to name his feelings

- Independence —the desire to do things on his own

- Beginning initiative—to start to do some things on his own without being told

Physical
- Jumps with both feet off the floor
- May pedal tricycle for short distance
- Balances on one foot for short period
- Draws circular scribbles and lines
- Helps with dressing and undressing self
- Starts to gain control of bladder and bowels but not consistent; "accidents" are common
- Aware of body functions
- Begins to use scissors

Cognitive: learning and thinking
- Repeatedly asks, "What's that?"
- Recognizes some shapes and colours
- Sometimes thinks that toys and objects are alive
- Sorts objects by colour and size
- Uses two- to three-word sentences
- Has a word for almost everything
- Understands *in, on* and *under*
- Is understood more by others
- Begins counting
- Knows own name

Emotional
- Tests limits set by parents
- Wants and needs to do things for self
- Sometimes wants to be *big* and sometimes wants to be *little*
- Poor impulse control
- Finds it hard to stop enjoyable activities
- Physical responses (like hitting or biting) decrease as talking improves

Social
- Dawdles
- Starts to pretend-play with others
- Likes to please others

Development: 3 to 5 years | The thinking stage

Tasks	Milestones
This is the **thinking stage**, a time when it's important for your child to keep learning about earlier tasks as well as: • Initiative— planning and acting on her own, without being told • Emotional regulation— how to cope and show feelings and emotions • Empathy— understanding how others feel • Capability— that she can do more on her own	**Physical** • Feeds self • Dresses and undresses self • Has bladder/bowel control day and night • Balances and hops on one foot • Throws ball (underhand and overhand) • Walks in a straight line, backwards and up and down stairs • Climbs on things (trees, furniture and playground equipment) • Kicks ball • Uses paints, scissors, pencils and crayons to purposefully create shapes, faces and letters • Can do simple chores with some help and direction **Cognitive: learning and thinking** • Always asks: "Why?" • Uses longer sentences for more detailed stories • Talks about the past and future • Improves grammar • Starts to understand difference between real and imaginary • Listens to and understands short stories • Sings simple songs and recites rhymes from memory • Has a very active imagination **Emotional** • More able to identify and name own feelings • Uses words more than actions to express feelings • Fears include real things (the dark, animals and thunderstorms) and imaginary things (monsters and ghosts) • Exaggerates and tells tall tales • Likes to talk about body functions • Develops a sense of humour **Social** • Begins to share and take turns • Hits less but name-calls more • Likes playing with other children • Uses imagination and themes in pretend-play • May have an imaginary friend • Likes to talk • Enjoys group activities and games

Tasks	Milestones
This is the **identity and power stage**, a time when it's important for your child to keep learning about earlier tasks as well as: • Identity—knowing who he is and how he fits into the world • Personal power—that he has control over his actions and can use it to get along with others • Industry—the ability to work on things from start to finish	**Physical** • More coordinated • Develops more complex skills • Muscles get stronger • Moves with more purpose and accuracy • Enjoys physical activity • May need more sleep due to demands of school **Cognitive: learning and thinking** • Greater attention span • Talks with more detail, using sentences and correct grammar • Says most words correctly • Tells longer stories on same topic • Tells stories with a beginning, middle and end • Likes telling jokes and riddles • Begins understanding death and asks many questions about it **Emotional** • Greater sense of right/wrong and societal rules • Begins to use *self-talk* to calm down • Dislikes being corrected • Easily upset by things that are unfair or "not right" **Social** • Becomes more competitive • Enjoys games with rules • Feels more empathy for others • Prefers gender-specific toys and playmates • Has a best friend • Other adults (such as a teacher) become influential • Likes to please

Infants
 BIRTH TO 6 MONTHS

*Making the decision to have a child—it's momentous.
It is to decide forever to have your heart go walking
outside your body.*

—Elizabeth Stone

Growing with your infant

Every new baby is a miracle. And nothing is more miraculous than the first six months of a child's life. Children grow and develop faster during this time than any other time. This is also the time parents and babies get to know each other and adjust to their new life together.

An infant is fragile in many ways and needs gentle care, kindness and patience. Looking after your infant's physical needs is essential—as is building your infant's trust. Your baby needs to know that you will care for and comfort her when she needs you.

From the beginning, infants can hear and see. They have reflexes for survival and are born with their own personality. Your infant soon reveals her own unique character and begins to form a deep bond with you. When you give your infant love, time and attention, she starts to recognize you and learns to trust you to be there for her.

From birth, your baby has a special language and sends you cues and clues about her needs. His first and greatest needs are for food, security, nurturing care and emotional connections.

In six short months, your infant's muscles become stronger and millions of connections form in her brain. As these things happen, she gains more control of her head, hands, legs and mouth. This is followed by learning to roll over and to sit up. By 6 months of age, she begins to reach out to explore her world.

For new parents, this stage can be joyous, confusing and exhausting all at the same time. Be patient. You and your baby are getting to know each other. Your loving care is your infant's most important need.

This chapter introduces you to your infant's body, mind and world in her first six months, and what she needs from you, her parents. For more on the detailed information on the care newborns need, see your copy of *From Here Through Maternity*.

Your infant's body

Your infant may lose some weight after birth, but should begin steadily gaining it after the first few days. Once babies recover their birthweight, they gain, on average, 180 to 240 g (6 to 8 oz.) a week for the first 2 months. From 2 to 6 months, weight gain averages 450 to 1,000 g (1 to 2 lbs.) a month. A baby's weight usually doubles by 6 months of age.

From birth to 2 months

At first, reflexes drive your infant's movements. She kicks, pushes her feet, grasps with her hands and turns her head to search for food or to make sure she can breathe. She can suck and swallow, and cries when she needs your attention. She doesn't know she can do these things—they are reflexes she is born with so she can survive.

You can expect your infant to sleep and wake often throughout the day and the night. At first, you may not see a sleep/wake pattern, but as she grows, your infant will settle into a more predictable rhythm.

Although your newborn's eyes can't yet focus, she scans your whole face by moving her eyes back and forth. She soon starts to follow moving objects with her eyes and by 8 weeks, her eyes can focus.

Infants have weak necks—both their head and neck need to be supported at all times. All babies are fragile and need to be picked up, carried and put down gently. Rapid movements, even playful bouncing, can be harmful.

Babies with normal hearing will wake, startle or respond to loud noises. Your baby can also make her own noises—crying, cooing and squawking— these are her way of talking to you. Responding to these first noises helps build trust with your baby and helps your baby develop speech and language.

At 3 months

By 3 months, your infant is more aware and interested in the people and activities around him. As he gets used to his surroundings and the routines of daily life, he begins to recognize you or others by cooing or becoming excited. He smiles with pleasure at people and may like or dislike his bath time. Now stronger, he begins to follow moving objects by turning his head.

From 4 to 6 months

From 4 to 6 months of age, your infant begins to hold her head more steadily. Once she discovers that she has hands and feet, she plays with and studies them endlessly.

By 6 months, most infants can roll, usually from their stomach onto their back, then from their back to their stomach. Many infants are able to sit at this age, although some support may be needed. At 6 months, your baby is also ready to start eating solid foods.

As your baby's babbling increases, she speaks more to people and toys. When you answer, she learns to take turns listening and responding. These are your infant's first conversations.

If you go to her when she cries, she learns to trust you to comfort her when she is upset. You begin to understand some of the things she likes and dislikes by the way she responds to them.

During this time, your infant starts to smile at familiar faces, laugh out loud and listen to her own sounds and babbles. She responds to your voice and is soothed by calm words or gentle songs. She can look and suck at the same time, but must stop and turn her head to listen. As your infant approaches 6 months, expect her to react to sounds even when she can't see what caused them.

Eating

Feeding your baby breastmilk

Breastmilk is the healthiest first food for babies—so healthy that Health Canada, the Canadian Paediatric Society and the World Health Organization recommend feeding only breastmilk to your baby until he is 6 months old; they also recommend babies continue to breastfeed once solid food is introduced.

Breastmilk is:

- A complete food. It contains just the right amounts of carbohydrates, protein, fat and minerals for your baby. It also contains growth factors, hormones and fatty acids needed for nerve and brain development. As long as you eat a well-balanced diet, the only supplement your baby needs is vitamin D. If you are a vegan, you or your baby may need additional supplements. Speak with a registered dietitian to be sure the nutrient needs of both you and your baby are being met.
- Easy to digest.
- Adjustable. Breastmilk changes to meet your growing baby's needs. Mothers who give birth to premature babies produce different milk than mothers who give birth to full-term babies. All mothers produce different amounts of breastmilk as their babies go through growth spurts.

- Protective. Breastmilk helps protect your baby from illness and respiratory and digestive infections. It may reduce the risk of allergies, diabetes, sudden infant death syndrome (SIDS) and childhood cancers. Breastfed babies are also less likely to be overweight as children or as adults. The longer you breastfeed, the better your baby is protected—and this protection lasts long after you stop breastfeeding.
- Convenient and safe. Breastmilk is available in the right amounts at the right temperature whenever your baby is hungry.
- Environmentally friendly.
- Free. Breastmilk is food produced from what you eat. To produce the best breastmilk for your infant, eat a variety of the food types recommended in Canada's Food Guide.

Breastfeeding is also:
- Good for mothers. Breastfeeding may help women lose some of the fat their bodies store during pregnancy. Working women who breastfeed tend to miss less work because their babies are sick less often. Breastfeeding decreases a mom's risk of breast and ovarian cancer and possibly type 2 diabetes—the longer you breastfeed, the lower your risk.
- Flexible. A nursing mother can express breastmilk (either by hand or with a pump), which she can refrigerate or freeze and give later to her baby by bottle, cup or syringe/feeding tube. See *From Here Through Maternity* for detailed instructions.
- Very workable. Even if baby or mom are sick or separated, breastfeeding can work.
- Supported. If you're having problems or are in a special situation, talk to your public health nurse or call Health Link Alberta for advice or for a referral to a lactation consultant if necessary.

The decision to breastfeed

Any number of reasons may affect your decision to breastfeed. To make an informed decision, consider all your options and talk to your doctor or public health nurse. Either can give you the most current information and sources of assistance. They are there to support you, no matter what decision you make.

Vitamin D

Vitamin D is an important part of your baby's nutrition. It helps the body absorb calcium and it prevents rickets.

Breastfed babies require a vitamin D supplement in the form of infant drops. If you are feeding your baby infant formula, talk to your doctor or public health nurse about your baby's specific needs for vitamin D supplementation.

Feeding your baby infant formula

If you are not breastfeeding, your baby needs iron-fortified infant formula for his first nine to 12 months. Iron-fortified formula comes in many forms: ready to use, concentrated liquid and powder. Always follow the manufacturer's instructions for preparing, using and storing infant formula.

If your baby is on powdered or concentrated liquid formula, follow the mixing instructions carefully. Adding too much water dilutes the formula and does not give your infant enough nutrients. Adding too little water makes the formula too strong and can damage your baby's kidneys. Before mixing powdered formula, prepare the water according to the manufacturer's instructions on the label. Be aware that powdered formula is not a sterile product. Prepare it carefully so that bacteria cannot grow.

Avoid propping a bottle in your baby's mouth or putting a bottle in your baby's crib. Always having liquids in the mouth increases the risk of choking and of cavities.

Babies need to have someone hold them when they are feeding. This physical contact gives them emotional warmth and a sense of importance and love.

Discard any infant formula that is left in the bottle after a feeding.

If you're having problems feeding your baby, talk to your doctor, public health nurse or call Health Link Alberta for advice.

What you can do: storing and preparing expressed breastmilk and infant formula

- Carefully follow the instructions for preparing and storing expressed breastmilk or infant formula in *From Here Through Maternity*.

- To warm bottles of breastmilk or formula, place them in a bowl of warm water. Microwaves are not recommended: they destroy some nutrients and the factors in breastmilk that help protect your baby from disease. Microwaves also heat fluids unevenly, which can cause serious burns to a baby's mouth. Also see *Food safety* on page 28.
- Always shake bottled breastmilk or formula to mix well; test the temperature on your hand or wrist (it should be body temperature, not too warm).
- Throw out any breastmilk or formula left in a bottle when your baby is done feeding. Do not re-use.
- Throw out worn or cracked bottle nipples, as they are a choking hazard.

When to feed

The feeding relationship is like any other relationship between a parent and child; each has a distinct role. The feeding relationship is important for healthy eating and it changes as your infant gets older. At this age, your role is to decide what to feed your baby and to follow her lead. Your infant's role is to eat and let you know when she is hungry and when she is full. The early months with your new baby are a time of learning for both of you.

The following are cues your infant is hungry:
- Searches with an open mouth
- Sucks on her hands or fists
- Smacks her lips
- Cries, although crying is a late sign of hunger and your infant may not be able to feed until calm.

Similarly, your baby knows when she's full. Pay attention and respond to her fullness cues. Stop feeding when she has had enough. This way she learns to listen to her fullness cues as she gets older. Some parents worry that they don't know how much their babies are drinking when breastfeeding. Trust your baby to take what she needs.

The following are cues your infant is full:
- Slows or stops sucking or swallowing after vigorously feeding
- Comes off the breast or bottle relaxed and content
- Puts up her hand to disconnect
- Closes her mouth
- Falls asleep.

Your baby's appetite may vary from day to day and feeding to feeding. She could eat quite a bit more during growth spurts (typically at the ages of 3 weeks, 6 weeks, 3 months and 6 months). If you are breastfeeding, you will notice that your baby wants to nurse more often for a few days. Relax, eat and drink well, and breastfeed when your baby tells you she's hungry. These frequent feedings increase your milk supply to meet your baby's growing needs.

By watching your baby, you can tell if she is getting enough to eat. She should feel heavier, steadily gain weight, have regular soft bowel movements and have six to eight heavy, wet diapers a day; her urine should be pale and odorless.

Excuse me?

No apologies are needed when babies burp. Burping helps them get rid of air bubbles in their tummies. If left there, the air can cause painful gas and bloating. You can help your baby burp in one of three ways:
- Hold him close to your body, facing over your shoulder (you may want to put a cloth on your shoulder in case he spits up milk). Gently pat or rub his back, starting from his bottom and moving up toward his head.
- Sit him in your lap, supporting his head with one hand under his chin. With the other hand, gently rub his back.
- Lay him on his tummy over your knees, support his head and gently rub his back.

Breastfed babies may not need to burp as often as they do not swallow as much air while nursing and have better control of the milk flow.

Feeding changes

An infant's diet goes through many changes. For the first six months, either breastmilk with vitamin D supplements or iron-fortified infant formula is all your baby needs for proper growth and development.

For the first eight weeks, infants can only take small amounts at each feeding, so they need to feed often. Breastfed infants need to feed at least eight to 12 times in 24 hours and may feed several times in a short period. This is called cluster feeding and it usually happens in the evening. Formula-fed infants take in about 60 to 120 ml (2 to 4 oz.) a feeding, six to 10 times a day. Because breastmilk is digested more quickly than formula, breastfed babies generally need to feed more often.

Over the next few months, your baby may feed less often and take in more at each feeding. Infants over the age of 3 months usually feed about six to eight times a day if they are breastfeeding. If on infant formula, they feed about five or six times a day, usually about 150 to 180 ml (5 to 6 oz.) a feeding. This is a general guide. Your baby is unique and may feed more or less. Your baby is getting what she needs if she is content and satisfied after most feedings, steadily gains weight and has enough wet and dirty diapers.

Babies need to eat day and night. Your infant feeds in her own way to meet her own unique nutritional and sucking needs. For the first six months, your baby is likely continue to wake during the night and needs to be fed when hungry.

While not on a set schedule, your baby does begin to have more predictable eating patterns. In these early months, she can suck and swallow liquids but is not able to safely swallow solids.

What you can do: breastfeeding and being apart

Breastfeeding can continue even when moms and babies are apart. Moms can:

- Express breastmilk, put it into well-labelled containers and refrigerate for feedings during the day. Your caregiver can give it to your infant by bottle or cup.
- Breastfeed more often at home.
- Discuss your baby's feeding with your caregiver and/or childcare or dayhome staff. Many offer nursing mothers and their babies a quiet and comfortable space for breastfeeding.
- Try to arrange your baby's feeding schedule so she is hungry and wants to feed when you arrive.
- Work out a plan, but be flexible.

When your infant won't eat

If you are concerned that your infant is pulling away too soon from the breast or bottle, is difficult to feed or is generally not feeding well, talk to your doctor or public health nurse.

If your infant is under 3 months of age, see your doctor right away if he:

- Refuses to feed, is fussy, does not settle between feeds, or wants to feed constantly
- Vomits most or all of a feeding two or more times in a row
- Is very sleepy or difficult to wake to feed
- Has fewer than six heavy, wet diapers a day
- Does not have a daily bowel movement in the first six weeks.

These are urgent medical concerns in infants under 3 months of age. Infants who are not feeding well can become dehydrated very quickly.

"Baby, this is solid food. Solid food, this is baby."

Around 6 months, introduce solid food into your baby's diet. Your younger infant may have a healthy appetite, but won't be ready for solid food until she's about 6 months old. Starting solid food too soon can cause choking, constipation or diarrhea, excess gas, and may increase the chance of developing food allergies.

Introducing food too early can also cause your baby to eat too much solid food and not take enough breastmilk. Studies show that giving babies solid food does not help them sleep through the night. There is no need to rush starting your baby on solid foods before 6 months of age. At 6 months, however, your baby is developmentally ready to begin solid foods and needs the added iron from her diet.

Your baby gives you cues that she is ready for solid foods when she:
- Has good control of her head
- Is able to sit upright in a highchair or infant chair
- Opens her mouth wide when food is offered
- Looks forward to eating with anticipation and excitement.

For detailed information about starting your baby on solid foods, see page 92.

Baby teeth and oral health

Your baby is born with teeth; they are under the gums. His first teeth usually start showing through the gums when he's around 6 months old, although some babies get them earlier and some get them later.

Many people think baby teeth aren't important because they fall out, but they are vital to your baby's overall health and development. Your baby needs these teeth to eat, to learn to talk, to hold spaces for his adult teeth and to build good self-esteem.

In short, your baby cannot afford to lose his baby teeth to cavities or injuries.

What you can do: keeping teeth healthy for life

- Look after your own teeth—studies have found that mothers who look after their teeth have children with fewer cavities.
- Avoid sharing spoons or cleaning soothers and bottle nipples in your mouth—bacteria that cause tooth decay can be passed from you to your baby.

- Start good oral health routines early. Even before teeth appear, gently clean your infant's gums every day with a clean, damp washcloth. When teeth begin to appear (around 6 months of age), you can gently clean your baby's teeth daily with a soft-bristle, baby-size toothbrush and water only. Toothpaste is not recommended at this age.
- Hold your baby when feeding. Avoid propping a bottle in your baby's mouth or giving your baby a bottle in bed.

When teething begins

Teething usually begins around 6 months of age, although some babies begin teething sooner and others later. Most children have all 20 baby teeth by 2 to 3 years of age.

Teething is a natural and temporary process, not an illness. It is normal for your child to be cranky, drool more or have mild, cold-like symptoms. He may also try to bite and put things in his mouth or change his eating and sleeping habits. Teething may cause loose bowel movements but does not normally cause diarrhea. If your infant has diarrhea, talk to your doctor.

When your baby is teething, avoid:
- Teething gels. These can harm your baby.
- Anything frozen. Babies can easily get frostbite.
- Liquid-filled teething rings. Your baby can choke if they break open.
- Teething biscuits. These are high in sugar and can cause choking.

What you can do: helping your teething baby

- Offer extra comforting and patience.
- Gently rub her gums with a clean finger.
- Provide a clean, damp, cold washcloth or clean, solid teething ring for baby to chew on.
- Talk to your doctor before giving your infant acetaminophen (for example, Infant's Tylenol).
- If your baby bites you when breastfeeding, take her off the breast immediately, gently but firmly say: "No." Offer the breast again,

but continue to take her off each time she bites. She will soon learn to stop biting.

For more information on your child's teeth and oral health, ask for a copy of *A Parent's Guide to Healthy Teeth for Children Birth to Six Years* from your public health nurse.

A few words on soothers

Babies suck to eat. Sucking is also a natural way for babies and young children to comfort themselves when they are tired or upset. Sucking for comfort may begin early in life and decrease as the child gets older. Your baby may suck on his thumbs, fingers or fists, or you may decide to use a soother. If so, here are a few things to remember:

- Many breastfed babies meet their sucking needs by breastfeeding.
- Breastfeeding should be well established before you offer your baby a soother.
- A soother does not replace feeding or comforting your baby.
- Choose a soother that is the correct size for your baby's age.
- Choose a one-piece soother with a soft, flexible nipple that flattens to the roof of your baby's mouth.
- Before using a soother for the first time, disinfect it in boiling water for one minute. Cool completely before giving it to your baby.
- Do not clean a soother by sucking on it yourself. This can spread germs that can cause tooth decay and illness from you to your child. Keep soother clean by washing it with hot, soapy water and rinsing after each use.
- Check your infant's soother regularly. Throw away soothers that are cracked, punctured or torn.
- Replace your infant's soother every two months, before damage occurs.
- Never tie a soother around a baby's neck. This can strangle a baby and cause death. Specially designed clips on short ribbons that cannot go around your baby's neck (about 15 cm or 6 in.) may be used to attach soothers to your baby's clothing.
- Never dip your baby's soother in sugar, honey or drinks containing sugar or alcohol. They can cause cavities and make babies very sick.

Sleeping

Nothing is more peaceful than the sight of a sleeping baby. Adults often look upon a baby's slumber with envy or say, "I slept like a baby" after waking up rested and refreshed from a good eight hours of sleep.

In truth, if all adults slept like newborn babies, they'd feel like the parents of most newborn babies—tired.

Infants have sleep patterns that are perfect for their needs and quite different from older children and adults. Their tiny tummies can only hold a small amount of milk so infants wake up to feed often—day and night. As they get older they are able to sleep for longer periods of time.

Although infants sleep about 16 to 18 hours a day for the first three months of their lives, they usually only sleep about two hours, and seldom more than three or four hours, at a time. When awake, your infant needs your attention through feeding, changing, comforting, holding, talking and playing.

Unless they are sick, babies are perfectly content with these sleeping arrangements. Parents, however, can find them exhausting. Babies' sleep patterns can continue this way for five or six months, although some babies may start sleeping longer at night by the age of 6 weeks.

Every baby's sleep pattern is unique. By understanding your infant's sleep/wake patterns and how they change, you can help your new baby learn good sleeping habits early on.

Your own sleep is important too. For more information about parents and sleeping, see *Caring for you* on page 79.

This way to sleep

Fussing, rubbing his eyes, pulling his ear, yawning, and faint, dark circles under his eyes are all cues your baby is tired and ready to go to sleep. The sooner you put him down to sleep the better. Waiting can result in an overstimulated or overtired baby who has difficulty relaxing and going to sleep.

It may take some time to learn your baby's sleep cues, patterns and rhythms. Until you do, expect your baby to be tired and ready to sleep after being awake for two hours for the first six to eight weeks of his life.

What you can do: learning night from day

Some babies seem to spring to life at night. In the first couple of months, your baby's schedule is your schedule. In the early weeks, you can help him learn the difference between night and day by:

- Keeping your home light and bright during the day; keeping lights dim or off at night.
- Not worrying about noises such as ringing phones, radios, TVs, dishwashers and doorbells during the day; turning these noises down or off at night.
- Playing during the day. Keep nighttime feedings quiet and voices and actions low so your baby learns nighttime is for feeding, then sleeping, not playing.
- Following your baby's lead. Most babies need to be fed during the night. Your baby knows when he needs to eat.
- Being consistent as your infant's sleeping/waking habits and patterns develop. As much as possible, have regular routines for bathing, playing, feeding and other activities when he is awake.

On their own

After the first few weeks, and given the chance, your baby may fall asleep on her own. Rock or nurse your baby to bring her close to sleep, then put her down when she's sleepy but still awake. "As early as 4 months of age, begin a routine of calming a baby into a quiet state, then put her down while she's still awake," says Dr. T. B. Brazelton. "This way she can learn how to put herself to sleep. She is then prepared, when she briefly wakens, to get herself back down to sleep."

It's not a problem if your infant falls asleep when you're rocking or feeding her. Rocking is a gentle way to comfort a baby. If your baby always associates rocking or feeding with falling asleep, however, she may come to need either or both of these things to be able to go to sleep—and you may be setting yourself up for problems later on. Babies learn from experiencing things over and over. When infants go to sleep and wake up in the same place, such as their crib or bassinette, they learn that this is where they sleep.

Your baby soon learns to trust that you will be there when she needs you. By learning to soothe herself, she also learns she can fall asleep on her own.

What you can do: teaching your baby to self-soothe

- Babies toss, move, waken and even cry during sleep. Before rushing to her side, listen to your baby's cry. (You'll soon learn the difference between a little whimper and an "I'm starving and want you NOW" howl.) See if your baby naturally falls back to sleep within a few minutes. Picking up and talking to a gently stirring baby can fully wake her.
- A soft blanket or sucking can also calm your baby.
- Some babies sleep better with soft background or white noise (it can filter sudden, loud noises). Special tapes and machines are available or you can quietly play static on a radio.
- It helps to remember that your baby will start to sleep longer as she gets older.

Safe asleep

When tired enough, people sleep almost anywhere, but when you put your baby down to sleep, the safest place is in a crib that meets current government safety standards.

A safe crib:
- Is made after September 1986
- Has slats that are no more than 6 cm (2-3/8 inches) apart
- Has a good condition, firm mattress that fits snugly in the crib frame
- Is free of pillows and heavy blankets that could cover baby's face
- Is free of toys, stuffed animals, bumper pads and positioning devices.

Your baby is not safe sleeping in an adult bed, on a sofa, waterbed or recliner, or on loose cushions or pillows. These places have hidden dangers: babies can fall, overheat, become trapped or be smothered.

Your baby is safest in his own crib, near you. Rather than share a bed with your baby, share a room; you can put your baby's crib in your room or put a bed or mattress in your baby's room.

SIDS

The unexplained death of an otherwise healthy baby when sleeping (under the age of 1 year) is called sudden infant death syndrome (SIDS). The cause of SIDS is unknown, and it can happen to any baby. Babies who sleep on their stomachs, babies whose mothers smoke and Aboriginal infants are more at risk for SIDS.

Since 1994, parents have been encouraged to put their babies to sleep on their back, and the rate of SIDS has dropped dramatically.

What you can do: reduce the risk of SIDS

You can reduce the risk even more if you:

- Always put your baby on his back to sleep. Make sure your baby's caregivers know to do this.
- Keep your baby away from second-hand smoke. Quitting smoking benefits both of you. If you can't quit, try to cut down, and smoke outside, away from your baby's window. Don't let anyone else smoke around your baby.
- Make sure your baby is not too hot. Infants are usually comfortable in the same amount of clothing as adults in the room.
- Put your baby to sleep in a safe crib, near where you sleep or breastfeed.

Is my baby sick?

You know your infant better than anyone and are the best judge of a change in his appearance or behaviour. While infants can be amazingly resilient, they can also get sick very quickly. Call Health Link Alberta or your doctor if you notice any of the following symptoms:

- Extreme changes in behaviour, especially if your infant becomes unusually quiet or irritable, very sleepy or weak
- Refuses to eat or eats poorly at two or more feedings
- Vomits forcefully (more than just spitting up small amounts of milk, which is normal)
- An increase or decrease in urinating (six to eight heavy wet diapers a day is normal)
- Constipation or diarrhea
- A fever (see *Taking your child's temperature* on page 37)

- A change in skin colouring
- Sweats a lot
- Noisy breathing or a cough that becomes worse
- Red, irritated and light-sensitive eyes
- Body twitches or shakes
- Screams, rolls head or rubs ears (these can be signs of pain)
- Poor weight gain (this is a more urgent concern if your baby is under 3 months of age. If this is the case, see your doctor right away).

See your doctor right away or go to your nearest emergency department if your infant is:

- Under 3 months old and has a fever
- Showing signs of dehydration (dark-coloured urine with fewer than four wet diapers in 24 hours; dry skin, mouth and tongue; or greyish skin)
- Sick and getting worse

Call 911 immediately if your baby is:

- Breathing slowly or with difficulty
- Limp or immobile
- Not responding.

Your infant's mind

An infant's mind is very active. The brain grows and develops rapidly in the first years of life as a result of what your baby experiences. What an infant senses (touches, tastes, sees, hears and smells), and how the people around her respond, forms the early brain connections for thinking and feeling.

We are just starting to understand why these early experiences and connections in the brain are so important. These connections determine how a child thinks, develops skills, learns how to cope and get along with others, and, eventually, even how she participates in community life as an adult.

Early brain development and growth depend on what scientists call *reciprocal sensory stimulation*. Fortunately, you don't have to be a scientist to understand what this means. It simply refers to the everyday two-way interactions that you have with your baby. Your baby's brain develops best

through her back-and-forth connections with you. This means that when you gaze at your baby and she gazes back, when you talk and she listens, when you listen to and imitate her sounds and expressions, when you touch and smell each other, you are making brain connections.

These exchanges happen hundreds of times a day, and they help your baby experience and process what is going on around her. Almost all parents and their infants are drawn to each other. It is nature's way of making sure babies survive. When these exchanges engage both parent and child, a solid foundation can form for future health and learning.

With the increasing importance being placed on these exchanges, parents are encouraged to make them often and to get help if they are concerned that their baby is not responding.

Making sense of the senses

When you share a gaze, point out pictures in a book, talk with and comfort your baby, you are putting his senses to work and building his brain connections. This activity helps your infant form a close relationship with you and teaches him about his world.

Vision

About 80 per cent of a baby's learning is through sight. Your child's eyesight is a precious sense that should be watched and protected.

Your infant's first eye examination should be at 6 months of age.

Babies with normal sight:

- Can see at close range at birth. Objects further than 25 to 35 cm (10 to 15 in.) are blurry. Newborns like high-contrast objects (black and white).
- Can follow objects with their eyes and start to turn their heads to follow moving objects by 6 weeks.
- Can focus on faces and can distinguish red and blue from white by 8 weeks.
- Have good control of eye movement by 4 months.

Signs of poor vision include:

- No interest in faces or toys suited to his age
- Eyes rove or jiggle
- Tilts head or squints
- White or strange light reflects from the pupil
- Pupil has unusual size or shape
- One or both eyes turns or crosses. *

*For the first six months, your infant's eyes may sometimes appear crossed or out of alignment. This is usually normal. If it is constant or continues after the age of 6 months, see your doctor right away.

Hearing

Babies can hear and listen even before they are born. At birth, their hearing is similar to an adult's. Babies learn by listening to sounds and voices. They learn to connect the sounds they hear with the people, animals, objects and actions that made them. This helps babies make sense of the world around them.

As your infant grows and develops, she uses her hearing to communicate and interact with others. The ability to hear is an important sense for developing normal speech and language skills. Even a mild hearing loss can affect her speech and language ability.

If your infant doesn't seem to respond to sound, if she makes fewer noises instead of more, or if you're concerned about her hearing, ask a public health nurse or doctor for a referral to an audiologist for a hearing test. The earlier hearing problems are found, the earlier treatment can begin. Hearing can be tested at any age.

Touch

Touch is the first sense infants develop in the womb. By birth, an infant is very sensitive to touch, especially around the mouth, palms of the hands and soles of the feet.

When you pick up, touch and comfort your baby (by holding or cuddling him, by reaching for his hands, gently rubbing his back or playfully counting his toes) you are giving him sensory nourishment and a sense of security, especially when your touch is combined with direct eye contact, or shared gaze. This direct connection actually allows your child's developing brain to learn from your developed brain. Touch is crucial to how a child learns to regulate his emotions and feelings as an infant and throughout his life.

Gentle touch and comfort help an upset baby settle and reduce stress. Experts in child development often describe this as lowering the thermostat of the stress response.

The amount of touch infants need varies. Some require more, some less. Some babies like long snuggles, others a quick cradle in your arms. You will quickly learn how your child responds to touch.

What you can do: engaging your baby

- Hold your baby in your arms, and look into his eyes; when he looks back at you, it may appear random, but if you look carefully you will see that he is scanning the edges of your face. This is how he gets to know you.

- Hold him close so he can feel and smell you.
- Rub noses and watch him respond.
- Repeat his sounds and wait for a reply. As he gets older, he will try to match your facial expressions too.
- Some babies need more stimulation, some need less. Experiment with your voice and gestures. Some babies respond better to a higher pitch of voice, or big facial expressions. Or you may need to lower the tone of your voice and use a softer, gentler approach. Try different things to see what works best for your baby.

How your infant communicates

Your infant communicates through movement, sounds, and with her eyes and face.

Expect your baby to begin making cooing sounds when she's about 2 to 3 months old. When you look right at her, smile and imitate her sounds, she learns that people take turns in conversation. When she says something and you copy her sounds, she learns what she's said is important and likely makes the sounds again. Such sound play is important in developing early words.

Although babies may seem to focus on sounds from a TV or a radio, they do not learn language from them. Your baby needs to see and hear you talk and needs you to respond to her first sounds and gestures.

Learning speech and language

Babies love voices—especially yours. The way you talk with and respond to your infant makes a big difference in his speech and language development. Simple things such as exaggerating new words, using simple sentences and talking face-to-face, help him learn language and become excited about talking. Your growing baby soon turns his head to look at you when you speak.

Children learn words and sentences by talking, singing, playing and reading with you. Your child gets much more from the sound of your voice and the time you spend with him than from fancy or expensive toys, flashcards and TV shows. Screens (TVs, DVDs, computers and the like) are not the best way for your child to learn language. You are.

Be patient. Listening, babbling and making sounds are the first steps in language development. Your baby begins to speak his first words around

12 months of age. Children under 18 months of age can understand more language than they can express.

Babies need and love lots of repetition. Music and games are fun—and make words easier to remember and language come alive for you and your baby. Babies don't need to understand the words for these moments to be learning experiences, especially when they're sharing them with mom, dad, grandparents or older siblings. Cuddle your baby as you share a book—it's never too early to read to your child.

What you can do: encouraging language

Engage
- Try different ways of holding and talking to your baby. Some babies need energetic conversations, some need gentle tones.

Talk
- Let your infant hear you—talk about what you do, see and hear. Tell him about your likes and dislikes.
- Add comments to your everyday routines to help your infant begin to understand words and ideas.

Read
- Read to your infant in a calm, soothing manner.
- Choose books that are colourful and safe to chew (cloth, plastic or heavy cardboard). Let your baby hold the book and play with it.
- Point to pictures as you name or describe them.

Play with language

- Use nursery rhymes and finger games (for example, *Round and Round the Garden* or *This Little Piggy*)
- For newborns and very young babies, try rhymes that involve gentle touch, such as patting their feet or gently moving their arms while you're talking (for example, *Pat-a-Cake*)

Sing songs

- Try upbeat and cheerful songs for play, soft and soothing lullabies for comfort.
- Forgot the words? Don't worry—make them up or check the Internet or a local library to refresh your memory.

Check out programs for parents and babies in your community. Your public library is a good place to start. Programs such as Story Time, Parent-Child Mother Goose, Literacy and Parenting Skills, Books for Babies/Jump Start and Homespun are a few examples.

Play and playing

As your baby grows and develops new skills and abilities, the way she wants to play with you changes. For the first month, your baby simply plays by watching you, following you with her eyes and listening to your voice. You are her favourite playmate!

The more you can play with your baby the better. While the best play is often unplanned, developing some routines is helpful. Follow your baby's cues. Taking turns during play helps your baby learn to respond to you. Taking turns is also the first step in learning to control movement and learning about the objects around her. At this age, your infant may not be able to take turns, but it's worth encouraging from an early age.

Watch for your infant's cues. When she is actively alert—smiling, cooing, looking engaged and interested—it is a good time to play. If she pulls away, looks frustrated or cries, she's had enough. Watch your baby and you soon learn her way of communicating with you.

There is no right or wrong way to play.

When children take the lead, they make amazing discoveries. Your child never outgrows the joy and pleasure of being able to pick and choose what she wants to do for at least part of her playtime.

Play is both simple and important. Playing with your baby builds a strong foundation for physical and social skills and for learning and thinking.

Give your baby safe toys

Keep play safe. Babies explore and learn with their mouths as well as with their eyes, ears and hands. As soon as they can reach things, they put those things in their mouths. Toys and toy parts should be large enough that they are not a choking hazard. Anything that can fit through a toilet paper roll is small enough to choke a baby.

Durable, washable toys are best for babies. Choose toys suited to your infant's age; these include:

- Mobiles
- Music boxes
- Pictures of faces
- Soft, safe, chewable books—cloth or board
- Baby's own hands
- An unbreakable mirror
- Soft, squeezable toys that make interesting noises
- Rattles.

Encourage movement

Infants need to kick and move to strengthen their muscles and learn about their world. Babies who lay or sit in one position with their head against something solid (like a high back chair or crib mattress) for long periods of time may develop a flat area on the back or side of the head called *plagiocephaly*.

To prevent plagiocephaly, change your baby's position often when you're holding her. Give your baby lots of tummy time during the day when she's awake and you are with her. Put her on her tummy or side on a clean blanket on the floor. She may not like it at first, so start with a few minutes and build the time slowly.

Tummy time helps your baby gain control of her neck and head, and encourages crawling. It is important to your baby's social, emotional and physical development.

Plagiocephaly (flat spot on head) can become permanent, so it needs to be treated promptly. Ask your doctor, public health nurse or Health Link Alberta for more information.

What you can do: developing play skills

Play face-to-face games

- Babies like to explore with their eyes and ears and are very interested in faces and voices.
- Games such as *Peek-a-Boo* help teach your baby you're still there even if she can't see you.

Take turns

- Examples of turn-taking play include making faces at each other, hiding toys under a blanket for your baby to find, and stacking blocks to knock down.

Follow the leader

- Follow your baby's lead. Give her a toy or object and see what she wants to do with it. Let her explore the toy for several minutes before you show her how it works.
- When your baby gets tired, turns away or starts to fuss, stop the play and let her rest. Follow her interest and needs.

Let your baby move

- Use baby equipment only for what it is intended.
- Take your baby out of her car seat when not travelling in a vehicle to give her time to kick and wiggle.
- Provide short periods of supervised tummy time throughout the day when your baby is awake and you are with her. Make it more interesting by getting down on the floor beside her and putting an object or toy just in front of her.

Feelings and emotions

Infants show different emotions in different situations. A well-fed, sleepy and comfortable baby is very peaceful. This satisfied state can quickly give way to frantic crying when a baby is hungry, uncomfortable or has a wet diaper.

By 2 months, your infant smiles and coos when he likes something. As his brain develops, he becomes more excited about people, toys and food.

Your infant also shows you when he's unhappy, for example, if he dislikes his bath, has to wait to have his diaper changed, or has to sit too long in his car seat or stroller.

Your infant has almost no ability to control his emotions and at times he will be overwhelmed, even with things that usually make him feel good. He needs your help to feel comforted, so he can eventually learn to do this on his own.

At this stage, your infant's emotions are expressed with three messages: "I like it," "I don't like it" and "I need you." As you get to know him, you will see that he gives you cues to tell you how he's feeling.

Your infant tells you "I like it" when he is quietly alert, looks relaxed, watches with interest, brightens and smiles. He tells you "I don't like it" when he puts his hands up, turns away, tenses his face and body, partly closes his eyes, wrinkles his nose or lip, or whimpers. Finally, he tells you "I need you" when he reaches for you, looks at or searches for you, leans or moves toward you, fusses or cries. These cues mean your baby needs your comfort, especially when he's sick, hurt or upset.

When you support your infant's exploration and play, and comfort and protect him when he needs it, you build a healthy attachment relationship with your baby. The more secure your child is in his relationship with you, the more his self-esteem thrives. Secure attachment (the emotional tie that helps your child know you will protect and comfort him) in your baby's first year is the foundation for all his future relationships and learning.

What you can do: regulating emotions

- When your baby says, "I like it," is a good time to play, talk, sing, read and have fun.
- When your baby says, "I don't like it," it is time to stop or change the activity or let your infant rest.

Follow your baby's lead. Limit the things he doesn't like as much as you can and stop when he tells you he's had enough.

- When your baby says, "I need you," it means he needs comfort. Go to him and pick him up, talk calmly and soothingly. You won't always be able to stop the crying, but you can always be there for him.

- Share in your child's happiness and excitement with smiles and encouragement.

- As much and as often as you can, show your infant your love, joy and other positive feelings.

- Let your infant explore his world and let him know that you will protect him.

If these feelings or actions of closeness don't come naturally to you, you are not alone—and help is available. You can talk to your doctor if you're concerned about your relationship with your baby or your mental health (for example, if you feel depressed or constantly anxious). Your child's social and emotional development can be severely affected by circumstances such as ongoing stress, family violence, neglect or abuse. If any of these are a problem for you or your family, call Health Link Alberta to get the help you need.

Parenting programs are for everyone. If you would like more information about parenting programs and resources that can help you build your relationship with your baby, call Health Link Alberta, or www.albertahealthservices.ca.

Crying

Crying is one way your baby communicates. It's normal and it's meant to get your attention. Babies cry because they need something: food, a diaper change, a cuddle or some comfort. They also cry when they don't feel well. Sometimes babies cry for no obvious reason.

Almost everyone has heard an infant cry, but as a new parent you'll soon learn that your baby cries differently for different reasons.

You can't spoil a baby by picking her up when she's crying. Crying infants who are consistently picked up and comforted in their first six months tend to cry less in the next six months of their lives.

What you can do: when your infant cries

Make your infant comfortable

- While all infants need to be handled gently, some like to be snuggled, and others like a looser touch. Find what works for you and your infant.
- Hold her close to your chest, skin to skin; your heartbeat may soothe her.
- Offer a favourite blanket or soft toy while cuddling.
- Check the back of baby's neck to see if she's too hot (sweaty) or too cold (cool to touch).
- Check baby's diaper; babies like to be clean and dry.
- Encourage your baby to suck.
- Give your baby a gentle back rub.

Use gentle motion

- Gently walk or rock with your baby. Use a baby swing if you have one; always fasten the safety strap.
- Take your baby for a walk in a stroller.
- Carry your baby in a sling or baby carrier.
- Some babies like to go for a car ride; make sure she's secured in an infant car seat.

Use sound and music

- Hum or sing a lullaby.
- Turn on a vacuum cleaner, clothes dryer or dishwasher; these sounds can sometimes calm a baby.

Check your environment

- Is the radio always playing? Is the TV always on? Are people always coming and going? Too much activity can overstimulate babies and young children, and lead to fussing and crying.
- Some babies thrive on activity; others find too much activity overwhelming and may need to move to a quieter place for a while. By watching your child's response, you'll soon learn what she needs.

The patterns of crying

All babies cry—some more than others. You may find that crying can be very frustrating. Understanding infant crying won't always stop the crying, but it can help you get through the first few months.

Research has shown the crying patterns of normal, healthy infants are very similar. Parents find it helpful to know that crying:

- Becomes more frequent when babies are 2 weeks old
- Peaks around 2 months of age and starts to decrease by 3 to 4 months
- Can come and go unexpectedly for no apparent reason
- Can sometimes continue despite the efforts of caregivers. Sometimes, babies just can't stop crying
- Can make healthy infants look as if they are in pain even though they might not be
- Can go on for 30 to 40 minutes or longer
- Occurs more often in the afternoon and evening.

Babies don't cry because they are mad or bad, they cry because they need something and they need you to help them. Sometimes infants can't stop crying or be comforted, no matter what you do. You are not a bad parent if your infant cries or can't stop crying. If you are worried about your baby's crying, talk to your doctor or public health nurse.

What you can do: when your baby can't stop crying

- Stay calm. Although they generally quiet when comforted, most infants have times during their day when they are unable to stop crying. Some babies cry more often and others cry for longer periods.

- If you find yourself getting frustrated or angry, put your baby in a safe place, such as his crib, leave the room and gently shut the door.

- Take a 15-minute break to give yourself a chance to calm down before trying to comfort your baby again. Letting your infant cry for a few minutes does not harm him, however, getting frustrated and shaking your baby can be deadly.

Colic

Long periods of crying—generally more than three hours a day and more than three times a week—are often called colic. Colic tends to follow the same pattern as normal infant crying. It usually: increases at 2 weeks of age; peaks in intensity around 2 months; and gradually decreases by 3 to 4 months of age.

It may seem as if colic will never end. If you think your baby has colic, see your doctor to rule out any medical causes and talk to your publc health nurse about feeding and coping.

Take good care of yourself, too—colic is very hard on parents. Try to get as much help as you can and keep responding to your baby, even if it doesn't seem to be working. He knows that you are trying. For ideas to help you cope see *Caring for you* on page 79 and *Balancing life as a parent* on page 11.

Never shake a baby

Frustration with being unable to comfort a crying infant is the most common reason given for shaking a baby. Make sure that everyone who looks after your baby knows to never shake a baby.

Plan ahead and find someone who can help you. Try to arrange for regular childcare so you can get some rest. Ask a trusted friend or relative to act as an immediate backup for times when the crying is too much for you to handle. Keep their phone numbers nearby. Remember, Health Link Alberta is available 24 hours a day, seven days a week.

Sometimes just talking to someone can be enough to get you through.

Your infant's world

Your infant's world revolves around you. She relies on you (and other caregivers) for absolutely everything. As you get to know each other, you will learn what works to meet her needs. By giving her time, loving care and protection, you will help her adjust to her new world. This also helps give her the safety, security and confidence she needs to explore and discover as she grows.

Getting along with others

Part of what makes your baby unique right from birth is the way she responds to the world around her. For example, some babies are quiet and seldom cry; others are more vocal and cry more often. Some babies never seem to hold still; others seem to be content to stay in one place. Some welcome anything new with smiles and excitement; others greet new experiences with tears and anxiety.

The pattern of a child's response to her world is called *temperament*. Everyone has his or her own temperament—even you. Temperament helps explain why children in the same family with the same parents act and react differently to the same things.

Child development experts often refer to three types of temperament:

- **Easy or flexible:** children with this type of temperament adapt quickly to change, are most often in a good mood and tend to show their emotions (both happy and sad) in a moderate way.
- **Slow-to-warm-up:** children with this type of temperament tend to take more time to adapt to change, often seem shy and show their emotions more mildly.
- **Intense:** children with this temperament have trouble getting used to any change, may get into a negative mood easily or have strong emotional reactions.

Many children have a mixture of these characteristics.

Your child's temperament is what it is—he is born with it. Your temperament may be very different from your child's. You can't change either one, but you can find different ways to work with your child's individuality. This means accepting the way your child is and also working out a good match between you and your child.

For example, if she has a hard time meeting new people and you thrive on it, you need to find a balance between your needs and your child's needs. Give her time to warm up to someone new; don't force her to go to someone before she is ready. Gentle encouragement and patience are what she needs.

Adjusting yourself to your child's temperament is called *goodness of fit*. While her basic temperament won't change, what your child experiences and how you respond can often change the way she sees herself and her world. Your understanding and willingness to work with your child show her she is accepted for who she is.

Protecting your infant

The arrival of an infant brings out a nesting instinct in many parents. They become very busy creating a safe and comfortable home and surroundings for their children. In this section we look at the many ways you can protect your new baby from illness, injury and harm.

What you can do: keep it clean

A little mess is fine, but infants—as all children—need a clean environment.

- At home, create a separate diapering area that is safe and well organized, near a sink, and away from where food is prepared, stored or eaten. It should be used only for diapering and cleaned regularly.
- Discard solid bowel movements in the toilet.
- Put soiled washcloths, cloth diapers and clothing in a covered diaper pail and wash them regularly.
- Put disposable diapers in a designated, covered garbage can or diaper pail and empty often.
- Keep diaper pails and garbage out of the reach of children.
- Wash your hands regularly; always wash your hands after changing baby's diaper, using the toilet, before holding an infant, before providing care, and before and after handling food. For more information on handwashing, see *Wash away germs* on page 33.

Preventing falls

Falls are the leading cause of hospital visits for childhood injuries. Kicking and squirming infants can easily fall off furniture and other raised surfaces, even before they can roll over. It can happen very fast—even when you are in the same room and even before you think your baby can't move very much. Always keep one hand on your baby when she is on a raised surface, even if she is strapped in. When your baby is in her car seat or infant chair, never put it on a raised surface, where sudden movements can cause her to topple over. The floor is the safest place.

What you can do: preventing falls

- Use both hands to pick up and carry your infant.
- Securely strap your infant into her carrier, stroller, carriage, car seat, high chair or swing every time you use them. Straps that go around your baby's waist and between the legs are safest. Babies can slide through waist-only straps.
- Do not use baby walkers with wheels. They are banned for sale in Canada.
- A safe diaper-change table has a safety belt or ledge at least 15 cm (6 in.) high. Even then, never leave your baby unattended. Keep at least one hand on your baby at all times when she's on a high surface.
- Avoid placing car seats and infant chairs on raised surfaces.

Preventing choking

Your baby puts anything he can reach and grab into his mouth. Make sure that anything he can touch is too big for him to swallow. Anything that can fit through the end of a toilet paper roll is too small for a baby or young child. Use recommended soothers and teething rings only. Never hang a string around an infant's neck—for any reason.

Car seats

By law, you must restrain your child in a car seat with a harness system every time she travels by vehicle until she weighs 18 kg (40 lbs.). Infants are safest in a rear-facing car seat appropriate for their weight and height until they are at least 1 year old and weigh 9 kg (20 lbs.).

Holding your baby, even when travelling at slow speeds, is not safe. Only an approved and properly installed car seat can protect your baby.

You can make sure you are using your child safety seat properly by following these steps:

1. Get ready—before you buy a seat, make sure it is CSA-approved and has not been recalled. Read all the instructions that come with your seat AND the instructions in your vehicle's owner's manual.
2. Secure the seat—use a seatbelt or a universal anchorage system (UAS) to secure a rear-facing child safety seat to the vehicle.

3. Buckle your child in—make sure your child is properly seated. Then securely buckle her in the seat with a secure shoulder harness and correctly positioned chest clip.

If you need help:

- Consult the instructions that came with your child safety seat AND the instructions in your vehicle's owner's manual.
- Once you have read all the instructions, take the Rear-Facing Child Safety Seat Yes Test (see *From Here Through Maternity*; if you do not have a copy, contact your community health centre).
- Call Health Link Alberta for information on car seat classes in your community, or if you have other questions.

What you can do: car seats

- Replace car seats that have been in a collision or are more than 10 years old.
- Avoid heavy clothing and blankets between your infant and the seat's harness straps—keep the straps as close to your baby's body as possible. To keep your baby warm, cover her with a blanket after she is buckled in the seat.
- Never leave your child alone in a vehicle.
- Use car seats for transportation only—take your baby out once you have reached your destination.
- Contact your public health nurse if you cannot afford a car seat.
- If your baby rides in a grandparent's, friend's or childcare provider's vehicle, show them how to use a car seat properly.

Sunscreen and insect repellent

Being outside is good for your baby; being in direct sunlight is not. Keep your baby in the shade. A hat keeps him warm in the winter and keeps out the sun in the summer.

Keep bare arms and legs covered when outside to protect your baby from the sun and insect bites. Use mosquito netting on strollers to keep out the bugs.

Do not use insect repellent or sunscreen on infants under 6 months of age. See *The great outdoors* on page 30 for more on protecting your child outdoors.

In other's care

Before leaving your baby in the care of others (relatives, friends or babysitters), make sure they know where you'll be and how you can be reached. Be sure to leave the phone numbers, your first and last name, your address and any other important information next to the telephone, where it is easy to find in case of an emergency.

Spend time with new caregivers before they care for your baby. Ask what they know about caring for children and if they have taken a babysitting course or early childhood training. Children should be at least 12 years old before they are left alone or in charge of other children. Young infants need care from experienced adults.

Make sure your infant's caregivers know to never shake your baby. Write out a list of ideas of what usually works to soothe your baby (see *Crying* on page 71). Leave instructions for feeding and enough breastmilk or infant formula in prepared bottles in the refrigerator. Your baby's caregiver needs to be assured that you will return if needed. Return home when you say you will. Also see *Childcare choices* on page 23.

As your infant grows

For more information on keeping children safe and healthy at any age, see *Your child's world* on page 23.

Caring for you

"The bond that links your true family is not one of blood, but of respect and joy in each other's life," wrote author Richard Bach.

Parenting is a lifelong learning experience of building respect and joy. For first-time parents, the learning curve in the first six months of parenting can be steep. The great news is you can learn as you go along and you learn something new with each child you have. No one expects you to have all the answers. When you don't have the answers or have difficulty coping, ask for help from people you trust: friends, family, neighbours and health professionals can all be sources of support.

You're going to have good days and bad days. Every parent does. Getting through the bad days and celebrating the good days help you learn, gain confidence and trust yourself. You quickly figure out what works and what doesn't work for you, your baby and your family. Other people may be only too happy to give you lots of information and advice, but let your own heart and experiences help you choose the best way to do things for your family.

Discovering a new normal

Starting this new relationship takes time and energy and will be your whole focus for the next few months. Be kind to yourself. Give yourself, your partner and your baby time to learn and adjust.

Expect your baby to cry, and that sometimes she will be unable to stop, no matter how hard you try. Your baby needs you to stay calm and continue to try to soothe her. It is more important for you to stay calm than for her to stop the crying. If you start to feel frustrated, place your baby in a safe place (such as her crib) and take a 15-minute break. Take a break, don't shake! See *Crying* on page 71.

Get some sleep

You can expect a lot of interrupted sleep for the first few weeks of your infant's life. (See *Sleeping* on page 58). As much as possible, try to sleep when your baby sleeps—day or night. A cool, dark room and a firm mattress helps you sleep more restfully, even though you may not be able to sleep for very long.

Keep lights, sound and movement at a minimum during nighttime feedings and diaper changes to help both you and baby get back to sleep more easily. Many parents find that having their baby's crib next to their bed for the first few weeks helps keep mom and baby close and minimizes nighttime disruption, while still providing a safe environment their baby.

Don't try to do too much

If you can't keep up with everything, then focus on what's important to you. Your house needs to be clean but it doesn't have to be spotless. The important thing is to have time to spend with your baby and your partner, as well as find time just for you.

What you can do: if you are breastfeeding

- Remember that babies need to feed frequently day and night and that eating patterns change over time. See *Feeding changes* on page 53.
- Breastfeeding is not always as easy as it looks—especially in the beginning.
- Feeding your newborn can take up to eight hours of your day. If you have no support, talk to your public health nurse. Many community programs offer support and services for new moms.

- Babies feed more often when they are going through growth spurts. More breastfeeding helps increase your milk supply.
- Accept as much support as you can. Family and friends are often waiting to be asked for help.
- Keep a list of ways people can help (for example, take your baby for a walk, bring over supper, pick up a few groceries). That way you can easily assign a task when someone asks.
- A breast infection can be very painful and make you sick. See a doctor right away if you:
  - Feel sharp stabbing pain in your breast(s) when you breastfeed.
  - Have a painful area that is red, swollen and warm to the touch.
  - Suddenly develop flu-like symptoms (aching muscles, fever and chills).
- If you are having trouble getting your baby to feed or you are not feeling confident, a public health nurse can help. Call Health Link Alberta for more information.

Expect the baby blues

Four out of five women who give birth or adopt a baby get the baby blues. The emotional ups and downs typical of the baby blues can make new moms feel overly sensitive, sad and tearful. If you find yourself crying for no obvious reason, you likely have the baby blues.

The main cause of the baby blues is hormonal changes. Baby blues usually last from 3 to 15 days. Most mothers feel better by the time their infant is 2 weeks old.

A newborn baby brings big changes for any family and it is common for one or both parents to:

- Feel emotional highs and lows
- Lack confidence in their new roles
- Have changes in their relationships
- Feel tired from lack of sleep
- Try to do too much too soon
- Feel irritable or tense
- Find it hard to concentrate.

These reactions are normal, but if they get worse or if you have concerns, talk to a professional counsellor, your doctor or public health nurse or call Health Link Alberta for advice.

Know the signs of postpartum depression

A case of the baby blues that gets worse or doesn't go away could be a sign of postpartum depression. Postpartum depression after your baby's birth or adoption is a serious health concern. About 10 to 15 per cent of mothers develop postpartum depression or anxiety. The symptoms can appear any time between one week and one year after baby's arrival, and can include:

- Anxiety and panic
- Feeling helpless or unable to cope
- Dramatic changes in your sleeping or eating habits
- Frightening thoughts or feelings
- Inability to care for or about your baby.

If you feel like this or are not at all enjoying being a new mother (or not enjoying your baby), you may have postpartum depression or anxiety. Treatment is available, and as with any illness, the sooner it's treated, the better.

A mom doesn't always recognize the signs, so her partner or others in her life need to be aware of the symptoms and be prepared to act. You can get help from your doctor, public health nurse or Health Link Alberta.

Remember dads get blue, too

New dads can also get the blues or depression as they adjust to life with a new baby. The first few months of a baby's life are physically and emotionally demanding for both parents. Although dads do not have the dramatic hormonal changes experienced by new moms, they often feel a loss of freedom and an increased sense of responsibility. These new pressures can cause dads to feel anxious, helpless and irritable.

New parents can support and care for each other by sharing their feelings and listening to each other's concerns. If things are not getting better in the

first few weeks, talk to your doctor or public health nurse. They are there to support your whole family.

Your mental health

Depression has many degrees and can occur at any time in life. It can range from feeling low to feeling you can't do anything at all. If you experience serious or ongoing feelings of the following at any time in your life, we urge you to seek help or advice from a professional counselor, your doctor, your public health nurse or Health Link Alberta:

- Unhappiness, feelings of worthlessness or helplessness
- Difficulty in making decisions or in being around people
- Changes in your sleeping and eating patterns and a decrease in your sex drive
- Self-blame, unreasonable guilt, suicidal thoughts, sadness, disappointment and/or emptiness.

What you can do: for you

New moms:

- Rest when your baby sleeps.
- Take parenting one day at a time.
- Ask for and accept offers of help.
- Say no to the demands of others.
- Limit your visitors.
- Arrange some time for yourself.
- Talk to someone who can reassure you if you feel like crying.
- Get fresh air if the weather permits.
- Be aware that mothering and fathering look very different. Partners need to support and learn from each other as they find their way.
- Drop into your local community health centre. In Calgary and the surrounding area, Alberta Health Services holds free weekly Early Start Parent Drop In times at most community health centres. They're a chance to meet informally with a public health nurse and other parents for information and support. You can even weigh your baby. Call Health Link Alberta for times and locations.

New dads:

- You may have different concerns than your partner and different ways of caring for your baby. Build your skills and confidence together—share and learn from each other.
- Give yourself a chance to learn and become confident in all the new skills you'll need. Take an active role in your baby's care. To help you feel more comfortable, try holding, bathing, talking or singing to your baby.
- Share the parenting. If your baby is breastfeeding, you can still take part in other aspects of your baby's care and in spending time with your older children.
- Be patient, give your partner extra love and support.
- Encourage your partner to rest when your baby is sleeping and try to get rest yourself—you'll need it!
- Go that extra step to share household chores.
- Limit visitor and their stays.
- Ask for and accept help from others.

New roles

Moms and dads grow into their roles differently. Many new moms have deeply protective feelings. Sometimes it takes dads a few months to feel the same way. As you grow into your roles, discuss your feelings and how you can both be involved parents.

It's true, moms and dads tend to parent differently. Watch a small child on his parent's lap. A mom is more likely to hold her child facing her, while a dad is more likely to turn the child around to face the world. Moms tend to focus on relationships within the home, dads on the child's relationships with the world. Dads often have more boisterous play with their youngsters, encouraging them to stretch their limits. Neither of these ways is more right than the other—they are just different—and both are needed.

As long as both parents provide safe and loving care, children learn from and thrive with a balance of these styles. Families with one gender-influence absent are wise to find this influence for their children elsewhere (for example, an uncle, an aunt, a grandparent, a trusted friend or a neighbour).

If your family chooses to have one parent stay home with the children, you may find you each have mixed feelings. Parents at home all day may envy the freedom of the parent who has gone out to work. Parents who work outside the home, on the other hand, may envy the time the other parent spends with their children. Sharing these feelings with one another removes the guessing about what your partner is feeling.

It's a delicate topic, but your sex life is likely going to change. It may take several weeks until a new mom is physically healed enough for intercourse. Your new roles and responsibilities can also create confusing feelings that can be difficult to talk about with one another. Keep your relationship affectionate and close (with or without intercourse) by having good communication and finding time for you and your partner to be alone together. Be sure to plan your birth control options.

It is true that "babies are born and parents are created." Worrying about parenthood can cause stress; learning to be a better parent can build confidence.

Think about your own parents and the kind of parent you want to be and remember that you have a choice in how you parent your children. Connecting with others can help you learn. Watch other parents you admire, take a parenting class, read a parenting book, join a support group or go online. These are all ways to help you become the kind of parent you want to be.

Above all, enjoy yourself and your children. Parenting can be filled with unparalleled rewards and discoveries.

Babies
6 TO 18 MONTHS

Babies are such a nice way to start people.

—Don Herold

Growing with your baby

The first 18 months of a child's life are a source of wonder. At 6 months old, your baby is still tiny and completely dependent on you, although becoming his own person and eagerly reaching out to explore the world around him.

From 6 to 18 months, your baby continues to learn, grow and develop at a rapid pace. At times, it seems as if he's growing up right before your eyes. In many ways, he is, but he's still long way from outgrowing you and he's still very much a baby.

Your baby is moving from mainly *being* to energetically *doing*. His ability to do more (recognize people, grasp with his hands, sit up, crawl, stand and eventually walk) leads to many new adventures and discoveries.

Babies learn in many ways at once. When you sit and read to your baby, he does far more than look at pictures. He learns language from your voice and love and trust from snuggling against your body. When you stop and listen to his babbling, he learns that people take turns talking. His first attempts to turn the pages help develop his small muscles and eye/hand coordination.

Growth and development continue to be a process of two steps forward and one step back. It's perfectly normal.

As a parent, you also grow and develop every day. You may also feel your progress is two steps forward and one step back. It's like that. Even if you have other children, you continue to learn about parenting because it's different with each child.

The more you understand and respect what's normal for you, your child and your family, the more support you can give your child through the important steps of early childhood. The more time you spend with your baby now, the more you will both be rewarded. Time, attention and love remain the most valuable gifts you can give your baby.

In this chapter, we look at how your baby changes from 6 to 18 months and how your relationship with him changes as he becomes more expressive, more mobile and more independent.

Your baby's body

By the time babies are 6 months old, most weigh twice their birthweight. By this age, or soon after, most babies can roll over and have discovered that their hands can reach and hold things. As babies begin to crawl, stand and walk, they realize that they are separate human beings. They go from being completely helpless at birth to being increasingly capable, courageous and totally interested in discovering their world by the time they are 18 months of age.

6 to 12 months

From 6 to 12 months of age, your baby's rate of growth depends on whether you breastfeed or formula feed, but generally, she gains about 400 to 600 g (1 to 1-1/2 lbs.) a month. By 1 year old, your baby weighs about three times her birthweight.

During her first weeks of life, most of your baby's movements are from reflexes. Now, as both her body and brain develop, she is increasingly able to connect movement and thought. Her progress continues to be from the top of her body down and from the centre out. This means she gains control of her head and neck first, then her arms and body, and finally, her legs and feet. She rolls over and sits up before she has control of her hands and fingers.

Your baby is now moving with purpose. At first, she bats at things she likes. As her hand control develops, she reaches, grasps and brings these things to her mouth to explore. Expect your baby to taste and chew on everything she touches—from her stuffed toys to the corner of your coffee table! As her growth continues, she starts moving her whole body, first by crawling and eventually by walking.

Babies can go from kicking their legs and arms one day to rolling over the next. As the muscles in your baby's shoulders, back and stomach develop, she starts sitting up by herself for a few minutes at a time, although at first she needs support. In the weeks and short months that follow, she begins using her legs and arms under her body to try to crawl forward or backward (on her tummy or bottom).

By 10 or 11 months, your baby learns a new game. She loves to pick things up and drop them—just to see them come back again when you pick them up.

Although you may not always find this amusing, it helps your baby learn that things still exist even when she can't see them (this is called *object permanence*). Playing this way helps her begin to learn that when you go away, you'll come back too.

You can expect your baby to make a mess as she begins to drink from a cup and eat solid foods. For babies, touching, squishing and dropping food is as enjoyable and necessary as eating it.

As your baby approaches her first birthday, she gets better at the things she's been learning since she was 6 months old. She now explores her world from many different angles: on her tummy and back, then sitting, pulling and standing up. She may take her first steps while holding onto you or your furniture.

Once your baby is mobile, she never seems to stay still. You need to be more attentive and watchful. Your baby's world is getting bigger and as she explores she faces increased chances of harm or injury. (See *Protecting your infant* on page 76.)

12 to 18 months

Your baby's growing body is like an engine that runs all the time. His rate of weight gain starts to slow after he's 12 months old, but his activity level speeds up as his curiosity and need to explore fuel his adventures. Some days, his physical energy seems boundless.

His big and small muscles develop together. As he gains more control of his big muscles and gross motor skills, your baby becomes very good at crawling. His ability to stand up on both feet is followed shortly by trying to move his feet forward.

Learning to walk is a huge accomplishment celebrated by babies and parents alike. While most parents believe babies should be walking at 1 year old, it is completely normal for walking to begin any time between 10 and 16 months. Like everything else, babies learn these skills a little at a time, in their own time.

When your baby pulls up on furniture and takes his first wobbly steps, you know that he will soon be ready to venture out on his own. Climbing may come before or after walking as your baby learns to move up and down as well. By 18 months, he may also move his body in time with music and squat to look at or pick up things.

Your baby is using his small muscles and developing *fine* motor skills when he grabs and holds things between his thumb and index finger, feeds himself with a spoon, drinks from a cup, stacks two or three blocks or objects on top of one another, or turns the pages in a cloth book.

Your baby loves to explore his own body and is able to point to his toes, nose, ears and eyes. For babies, touching all parts of their body—including their genitals—is a natural way to learn about themselves. This comes hand in hand with your child's desire to dress and undress himself—a reflection of his growing abilities and independence.

Eating

At 6 months of age, your baby still gets most of her nourishment from breastmilk or formula but she is now developmentally ready to start on solid foods.

By 9 to 12 months old, your baby should be eating a variety of foods from the four food groups (grains products, meat and alternatives, milk and alternatives, vegetables and fruit) every day.

By 18 months, your baby should be eating a variety of foods at three meals and three planned snacks throughout the day.

Be patient in helping your child discover new food and your family's eating habits and traditions. Developing good eating habits and setting a good example are more important than making her eat pureed cauliflower. With time, your child learns how and what to eat by following your example.

Feeding your baby breastmilk

The World Health Organization and Health Canada recommend that babies be fed only breastmilk for their first six months. At 6 months of age, your baby is likely nursing about five or six times a day. Solid foods need to be introduced now to meet your baby's growing nutritional needs. With the addition of solid foods, breastfeeding can continue until children are 2 years old or older. The longer you breastfeed, the more your baby and you benefit.

Breastmilk continues to be a valuable source of nutrients and antibodies for your growing baby. Breastfeeding works best when you feed your baby when he wants to be fed. This way, your milk supply adjusts to meet his needs.

By this age, your baby has likely settled into a predictable pattern of nursing, although you may find he needs to feed more often for several days when going through a growth spurt.

Weaning

Listen to your baby and trust your own instincts when deciding when to wean from breastfeeding. Weaning is usually more comfortable for you and easier for your baby if it's mutual and gradual.

When baby stops breastfeeding

As babies grow and become more interested in their surroundings, they seem to be less interested in breastfeeding. If your baby suddenly refuses to breastfeed, look for possible reasons why, such as teething, illness or even something as simple as not liking your new perfume. This may be what's called a nursing strike. It's generally temporary and does not always mean your baby wants to be weaned. Baby-led weaning usually happens before children are 1 year old or after they're 3 years old.

If you're not ready to wean but your baby refuses to breastfeed, you can encourage continued breastfeeding by:
- Keeping feeding times quiet with no distractions
- Increasing cuddling and soothing
- Feeding your baby when she wakes up hungry in the night
- Offering the breast when baby is sleepy.

You may need to pump your breastmilk and offer it in a cup or bottle until your baby wants to resume nursing.

When mother stops breastfeeding

If you're ready to start weaning, offer your breast only when your baby shows interest. As your baby reduces the number of feedings per day, you may need to express a little milk for comfort until your milk supply adjusts and decreases. Talk to your public health nurse if you are concerned.

Gradually decrease the number of times a day you breastfeed, replacing those feedings with infant formula or, depending on your baby's age, whole fat milk (next page).

Begin using another feeding method (cup or bottle) at one feeding a day. Once your baby adjusts, replace a second feeding in the day. Cuddle your baby and give her your attention in other ways when you would usually breastfeed (for example, read a story). Your baby still needs to suck and may find comfort sucking her hands, her fingers or a soother. Bedtime and naptime feedings are often the last to stop.

Emergency or rapid weaning

Many mothers feel that if they or their babies are sick or must be separated for a long time, breastfeeding must be greatly reduced or stopped altogether. In fact, breastfeeding can be accommodated in nearly any situation. A hospital or community lactation consultant can advise how.

If you must rapidly wean, it may help to:
- Wear a supportive bra.
- Apply cold compresses (a bag of frozen vegetables wrapped in a thin towel) often to relieve breast fullness.
- Avoid using heat on your breasts.
- Allow your breasts to leak milk while showering; express or pump a very small amount of milk for comfort as needed.

Your breasts may soften but continue to produce milk for several weeks after breastfeeding stops. Talk to a lactation consultant. In the hospital, ask for a referral; in the community, call Health Link Alberta for more information.

Feeding your baby formula

Babies on infant formula generally feed three to four times a day when they are 9 to 12 months old; about 180 to 240 ml (6 to 8 oz.) each feeding.

If you decide to formula feed, iron-fortified formula is recommended for your baby's first year. Pasteurized, whole-fat cow's milk (homogenized or 3.25% milk fat) can be started when your baby is 9 to 12 months old once your baby is eating a variety of iron-rich foods with most meals.

Starting solid foods

Eating solid food is very different from breast or bottle feeding. It takes time for babies to learn to eat from a spoon. You can help your baby by first putting a little breastmilk or infant formula in a spoon and offering it to her. As she gets used to eating from the spoon, you can gradually add a little infant cereal or pureed iron-rich food. Mix it to a runny consistency for the first few days, then gradually thicken it as she gets used to the texture.

Offer your baby foods that are rich in iron after breastfeeding or formula-feeding. Examples of good starter foods are iron-fortified dry infant cereal (mixed with breastmilk, formula or water as directed on the package), cooked, pureed meat or poultry; and cooked and strained egg yolk, kidney beans or lentils. The order in which you introduce them is up to you; all these foods are rich in the iron your baby needs at 6 months. Add new foods one at a time, waiting at least two days between new foods.

Your baby's food can be homemade or store-bought; it does not need added salt, sugar or seasonings. See *Foods to avoid* on page 29 for foods not recommended for young children.

Always feed your baby solids from a spoon. Runny, solid foods (such as infant cereal) should never be given in a bottle as this may cause choking. Avoid the temptation to share a spoon with your baby; this spreads germs that cause tooth decay and illness from you to your baby.

Sit your baby straight up in a high chair, facing you when you feed her. This lets you see and respond to her cues and it also prevents choking.

If your baby makes a face when you feed her, it doesn't necessarily mean she doesn't like the taste. It's all a matter of learning how to use her mouth, tongue and throat in a new way.

Touch and feel help your baby learn about food and eating. As soon as she shows interest, let her try to feed herself—she will start with her fingers and hands before she tries to hold a spoon.

Your baby might have loose (but not runny) or more solid bowel movements when solid food is first started. Food sensitivities and allergies can occur almost immediately or a few days after a food is introduced. Watch for diarrhea, excessive gas, excessive crying, vomiting or a mild redness or roughness on baby's face or body.

What you can do: introducing new foods

The following are general guidelines (adapted from The Canadian Paediatric Society) for introducing new foods to children of all ages:

- Start one new food at a time.
- Serve a new food with familiar foods.
- Encourage your baby to taste a new food but do not coax her to eat it. If the new food is rejected, accept the refusal calmly and try again another time. As new foods and new tastes become more familiar, children become more adventurous.
- Let children explore. The more they know about a food, the more they will enjoy eating it. At this age, knowing about food means feeling it and tasting it. As your child gets older, you may want to help her learn about where her food comes from or how it is grown or prepared.
- Be a role model. If your baby sees you and other adults enjoying foods, she's more likely to try them.

Iron-rich foods

At 6 months of age, your baby is developmentally ready to start on solid foods and he also needs the added iron from those sources in his diet for healthy growth.

When introducing iron-rich foods (cooked and pureed meat, poultry, fish, tofu, beans, cooked egg yolk, or iron-fortified infant cereal), begin with 5 ml (1 tsp.) mixed with breastmilk, infant formula or water to a runny consistency. When making iron-fortified infant cereal, follow the directions on the package label.

Swallowing solids is different from swallowing milk and you may have to try several times before your baby figures it out. As your baby gets used to this new way of eating, gradually thicken the mixture (see also *Food textures*, next page).

Babies

Vegetables and fruit

At first, cook and puree your baby's fruit and vegetables. Start with 5 ml (1 tsp.) a day and gradually increase the amount. To help your baby's body use the iron from his food, serve fruit and vegetables high in Vitamin C, such as: mangos, squash, sweet potatoes, green beans and broccoli.

Grain products

Start with single grain infant cereals before adding mixed grain cereals. As your baby progresses, add other grain products such as cut-up pasta, rice, couscous, unsweetened breakfast cereals or strips of toast.

Milk and alternatives

Once your baby is eating a variety of iron-rich foods, vegetables and fruit, you can introduce small amounts of plain yogurt or pasteurized soft cheese. As your child gets used to these dairy products, you can slowly add other types of cheese. Do not use yogurt and cheese labelled diet, light (lite) or low-fat at this age.

When your baby is 9 to 12 months old, you can give her pasteurized, whole fat cow's milk (also called homogenized or 3.25% milk fat) as long as she's eating a variety of other solid foods right for her age. Use a cup for drinking and start with very small amounts.

Wait until your child is at least 2 years old before giving her fat-reduced milk (2%, 1% or skim).

Avoid soy or rice beverages or other vegetarian drinks in the first two years. They may not contain enough protein, fat or calories for your baby to grow. Use soy formula only on the advice of your doctor.

Facts on fats

Babies need *good* fats in order to grow and develop. Good fats are found in foods such as whole-fat milk and whole-fat milk products, meat, poultry and fish. When choosing fish, select char, herring, mackerel, salmon, sardines, trout or light tuna. Other fish may contain high levels of mercury, which can harm the developing brains and nervous systems of young children.

What you can do: a new way of eating

Allow your baby to take the lead when eating:
- Wait for him to open his mouth when you offer food.
- Let him eat at his own pace.
- Babies can't help but make a mess as they learn to feed themselves. It's all part of the learning process.

He uses his hands first and then learns to use a spoon and cup with your help and patience.

- Help your baby learn that his body tells him when he is hungry and full. Stop feeding when your baby has had enough. Do not force your baby to empty a bottle or finish the food on his plate. This is the way he learns to stop eating when his body tells him he's full.

- Keep trying. If your baby turns new food down, wait a few days and try again.

- Have fun! Mealtimes are more than just eating. Babies are also learning family, social and cultural routines and traditions.

Food textures

Babies don't need teeth to start on solid foods. As a general guideline, start with strained, pureed or smooth food.

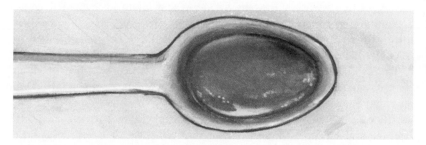

After a couple of weeks, once your baby is swallowing well, it's time to move to mashed and lumpy food. Progress to minced, grated, and finely chopped food and once your baby is eating these well, include diced and cubed foods.

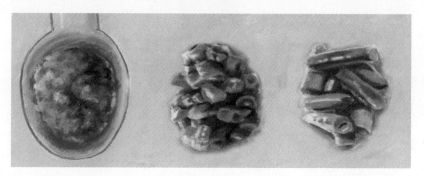

As babies get older, they need food with a greater variety of textures to help them learn how to chew. The mashed food stage is particularly important. If you wait too long to introduce it, your baby may refuse different textures of food.

Babies don't always like new tastes and textures. Forcing a child to eat can make her dislike her food even more and can lead to battles over food. Be prepared to offer a new food several times before your baby accepts it. Your baby's food likes and dislikes can change from day to day.

Drinking from a cup

Breastmilk or infant formula is still the only fluid your baby needs, although you can offer small amounts of water or juice (about 125 ml or $1/2$ cup a day) after your baby is 6 months old.

If you think your baby is thirsty, try offering a little water in a cup. This helps your baby get used to the taste of water. Water should not take the place of milk in your baby's diet. Remember—milk for meals, water for thirst.

Start with small amounts. It takes time for your baby to learn to use it, but getting him used to a cup helps him gradually give up his bottle.

Weaning from a bottle to a cup should take place by 12 to 14 months of age. Leaving it longer than that can make it more difficult for your child to give up his bottle later on.

Babies don't need juice, but if you decide to give it, choose 100% unsweetened, pasteurized fruit juice. Giving your infant juice can reduce his appetite for breastmilk or infant formula, especially if he sips it all day. Offer juice as part of a meal or snack. Avoid drinks labelled *beverage, punch* or *cocktail*, which are sugary drinks containing little or no actual juice.

Cups with sippy lids can prevent spills, but if used constantly throughout the day, can be bad for babies' teeth. Constantly sipping on a cup filled with anything but water means a sugar is always in your child's mouth and this greatly increases his risk of tooth decay. Prevent the mess that comes with learning to use a cup by limiting the amount you put in an open cup. A little at a time is all your baby needs.

Finger foods

Finger foods are foods your baby can pick up by herself and put in her mouth. They should be healthy choices, low in sugar and salt. Be careful with foods that can cause choking or cavities.

Recommended finger foods include:
- Soft, ripe, peeled fruit (such as bananas, pears, peaches, plums, cantaloupe or kiwi) cut into bite-size pieces or strips
- Cooked vegetables (cut into bite-size pieces or strips)
- Dry toast strips, bread crusts, bread sticks, bagel pieces, plain rice cakes and unsalted crackers
- Cubed or grated cheese
- Cooked tofu, beans or other legumes
- Mashed potatoes, cut-up casserole or spaghetti and tomato sauce.

Food safety

If using commercial or homemade baby food, don't feed your baby from the jar. Put the food you think your baby will eat in a dish and return the jar to the refrigerator. Always use a clean spoon to feed your baby. Throw out any leftover food that has touched the feeding spoon or baby's mouth.

Be very careful heating baby food in a microwave. Microwaves heat food unevenly and can form hot spots that could burn your child. Stir food well and test the temperature on your wrist before serving to your baby. Use only microwave-approved containers, wraps and lids. To prevent choking and illness, see also *Foods to avoid* on page 29.

Food for thought

- Eating becomes much more social for your baby as he joins in family meals at the table.
- In many cultures, food may be introduced in different ways. All foods can fit into a healthy diet. Talk to your doctor or public health nurse to make sure your baby's nutritional needs are being met.

- You and your child have different roles in feeding. Your job is to provide regular, balanced meals and snacks and a good example to your child. Your child's job is to decide how much to eat and whether he will eat. See *The feeding relationship* on page 122.
- Avoid using food as a reward and never deny your child's basic food needs because of unacceptable behaviour.
- Turn off the TV and loud music at mealtimes—too much activity distracts your child from eating.

Teeth and oral health

Between 6 months and 3 years old, all 20 of your child's baby teeth will appear. Baby teeth are important, and children cannot afford to lose them to decay or injuries.

Tooth decay in children is a painful bacterial infection that is the most common chronic childhood disease. It usually affects the upper front teeth and can spread very quickly. Tooth decay can affect your child's sleep, learning and eating. And it can result in tooth loss and surgery.

To keep baby teeth healthy, avoid putting your baby to bed with a bottle, propping a bottle for feeding, and constant sipping from a bottle or no-spill cup during the day. Wean your baby from a bottle by 12 to 14 months of age.

All foods, even nutritious foods, have natural sugars that can contribute to cavities. Start good eating habits early. Make healthy food choices for meals and snacks. If you give your child an occasional sweet treat, serve it with meals or when you can brush her teeth right after. Limit juice. Regular brushing and flossing are the best ways to prevent cavities. Brush and floss your child's teeth—young children are not able to effectively clean their own teeth.

What you can do: keeping baby teeth healthy

- Wash your hands and your baby's hands before any oral care.
- Before teeth appear, wipe your baby's mouth and teeth at least once a day with a clean, damp washcloth.
- When teeth appear, begin brushing twice a day with a soft-bristle, baby-size toothbrush and water only. Brush gently and thoroughly on the chewing surfaces, and along the gums—where teeth and gums meet.

- Rinse toothbrushes with water and allow to air dry in between brushing. Store safely out of the reach of your child and as far away from toilets as possible.
- Replace toothbrushes every three months.
- *Lift the lip* and start regular dental visits (see next page).
- Reduce the risk of passing cavity-causing bacteria to your baby and set a good example by keeping your own mouth healthy. Brush and floss daily and visit your dentist regularly.

Toothpaste

Until your child is 3 years old, brush his teeth with water only. Avoid using any kind of toothpaste unless recommended by your dentist or dental hygienist. Children this age are unable to effectively spit and may end up swallowing the toothpaste. Swallowing too much fluoridated toothpaste can lead to *fluorosis* (permanent white marks) on adult teeth.

Ask your dentist or dental hygienist if you have concerns about your baby's teeth and oral health.

Using dental floss

Flossing gets rid of food and plaque buildup between your baby's teeth. Once teeth appear, begin flossing as part of daily oral care.

Step 1
Take a piece of floss as long as your child's arm. Wrap floss around your middle fingers leaving about 50 mm (2 in.) of floss between hands. Using your index fingers, guide the floss between the teeth.

Step 2
Wrap floss in a "C" shape around the base of the tooth, where the tooth meets the gums.

Step 3
Starting at the gumline, wipe the full edge of the tooth with the floss, two to three times. Floss both sides of each tooth as well as the back of all of the molars. Change to a new section of floss as you move to each tooth.

Lift the lip

Be on the lookout for the first signs of tooth decay. Once a month, after brushing your baby's teeth, gently lift your baby's upper lip and examine her top and bottom teeth. If you see:

- Healthy teeth and gumline (smooth and evenly coloured) continue daily cleaning or brushing and flossing; visit a dentist by baby's first birthday or within six months of the first tooth's appearance.
- Whitish lines along the gumline, visit a dentist as soon as possible. This could be the start of tooth decay.
- Brown areas or black spots (cavities) along the gumline, visit a dentist immediately.
- Severe decay or broken tooth enamel, visit a dentist immediately.
- Red and swollen cheeks or gums, see a dentist as soon as possible.

Your baby will eventually lose her first set of teeth once her adult teeth come in, but she will keep the healthy habits you establish for regular dental care for life.

Baby's first checkup

The Canadian Dental Association recommends a child's first visit to a dentist take place at 12 months of age, or within six months of his first tooth's appearance.

The goal is to visit the dentist before your child develops any problems. Regular visits help:

- You learn how well you're brushing and flossing your child's teeth
- Your dentist find and fix problems early
- Your child learn that regular visits to the dentist can prevent problems.

If you're concerned about the cost of visiting a dentist, professional dental care is available at a reduced cost from Alberta Health Services. For more information, call Health Link Alberta.

Sleeping

Between the ages of 6 and 12 months, babies begin to sleep more predictably, sleeping more at night and less during the day.

At 6 months, most babies sleep for at least five hours at night and for as much as 11 hours at a time. Every baby is different and some may still wake to feed, but you should notice your baby gradually sleeps for longer periods at night. By 12 months, babies usually sleep for 11 to 12 hours at night and nap twice during the day (morning and afternoon). By 18 months, many babies give up their morning nap for a longer nap in the afternoon.

The myth of sleeping through the night

Parents dream and even boast about babies who sleep through the night, but for the first year, it is completely normal for your baby to wake up during the night.

Indeed, no one—baby, child or adult—sleeps through the night without waking. As adults, we wake several times a night to change position, pull up a blanket, check the clock or use the bathroom. Then we go back to sleep because we've learned how. Your baby can also learn, with your help, to fall asleep after waking in the night.

A calming routine

A calming bedtime routine helps your baby wind down at the end of the day. A routine might include: a relaxing bath, cleaning gums and teeth, getting into pajamas, snuggling with mom or dad for a lullaby or a story, followed by bedtime and lights out. Every family is different—find what works for you and your baby.

Routines help your baby know what to expect and increase his sense of security.

Self-soothing

If your baby always associates feeding, a soother, rocking, patting or a car ride with falling asleep, she may come to expect it when she wakes in the night. Your baby is able to learn ways of soothing herself. She may do this by sucking her thumb, rubbing a blanket or cuddling a soft toy.

Babies wake more easily as they go into the REM (rapid eye movement) stage of sleep. This can happen as often as once an hour while they are sleeping; self-soothing can help both you and your baby get better sleep.

Avoid the urge to pick up or soothe your baby every time she makes a sound or gently fusses in the night. Give her a few minutes to see if she settles on her own, then go to her if she sounds fully awake.

A nightlight may help a baby who seems to be anxious about being alone. It also makes it easier for you to move about in the room at night.

Naptime

Naps—short periods of sleep during the day—are not the same for every baby, but they tend to follow a general pattern. Between 6 and 18 months, most babies nap twice a day for one to two hours at a time. Your baby benefits from a nap in midmorning and early afternoon. Somewhere between 1 and 2 years old, your baby may give up morning naps.

Your baby gives you cues that he is tired and is ready for a nap when he:
- Loses interest in people or toys
- Fusses, yawns or rubs his eyes

- Looks glazed or quiets down
- Lies down.

If you wait too long to get your baby off to sleep, he may become overtired and be unable to settle down. He may seem to find new energy and want to play instead of sleep, only to become fussy later on.

Naps are important to your baby's good health and happy mood. As your baby gets older, he gets more of the sleep he needs at night and takes fewer and shorter naps.

A waking baby

Even when your baby starts sleeping all night, patterns can change. If your baby starts waking again in the night, it could be due to:
- Teething
- A growth spurt
- Illness
- Separation anxiety (see page 113)
- A change in your family's routine.

Disruptions to a baby's usual sleep patterns are most often temporary and best dealt with by patience and comfort. Once the cause of the disruption passes, it may take a few days (or sometimes weeks) for your baby's previous routine to return.

Planning for sleep

Some parents turn to sleep plans to help their babies learn to get to sleep on their own. A sleep plan is simply a set of guidelines that parents can follow to help shape their child's sleep. These methods range from gradually reducing your presence, to completely ignoring a baby's distress and letting him "cry it out". This last method is not recommended by Alberta Health Services. In making your choice consider the source of the advice and your baby's needs for comfort and security.

Sleep plans can be used with babies over 6 months of age, as long as they are in good health and their parents are not under unusual stress. You don't need to use a sleep plan if you and your baby are happy with your sleep arrangements.

If you choose to use a sleep plan, it is wise to plan ahead. Talk to other family members about when you will start it and how you will follow through. Be sure you can live with your plan (and your baby's crying) and only start when you know you can afford to lose a few days' sleep and can give extra attention to your baby during the day.

Your baby will likely fuss (sometimes a lot) when you start a sleep plan. The fussing should decrease nightly as you follow through with the plan. Using a sleep plan (and the crying that can result from it) doesn't harm older babies as long as their overall relationship with their parents is warm and nurturing. Avoid sleep plans that recommend completely ignoring your baby.

No baby should be left to cry for long periods.

For more information on sleep plans and healthy sleep, talk to your public health nurse.

What you can do: healthy sleep

- If you don't already have a bedtime routine for your baby, now is a great time to start. By following the same routine every night, your baby learns the signs of bedtime. You don't need a rigid schedule, but try to follow the same general pattern whether mom, dad or grandma put baby to bed.

- Your baby's unique personality and temperament may affect his need for sleep. Try to find the pattern that best suits him.

- Planning your routine around your baby's naps helps him develop better sleep patterns and ensures he gets the sleep he needs.

- If you are exhausted by your baby's nighttime waking, try to sleep during the day when your baby naps. You can also ask family or friends to relieve you for a few hours. Your sleep and health are important too.

- When your baby tries to stand in his crib, move the mattress to its lowest level so that he can't climb out.

Your baby's mind

Your baby continues to explore and learn about her world through what she sees, hears, touches, feels and tastes. Anything your baby can grasp goes into her mouth, whether she is hungry or not and whether it is food or not. The more she listens to and tries to say words and sounds, the better she becomes at speech and language (both now and throughout her life). As she learns to *read* the feelings and emotions of the people close to her, she starts to understand her own feelings and emotions.

You know your baby best. If you are concerned about her hearing, vision or how she responds to you or others, talk to your doctor or public health nurse. The earlier developmental problems are treated, the better it is for your child and family.

Vision

As your baby's vision gets stronger, you will see that he starts to notice the world around him. By 6 to 8 months old, your baby's eyes should focus equally. Your baby's first eye examination should be at around 6 months of age (see *Vision* on page 63).

Between 12 and 18 months, babies' eyes start to work with the rest of their body, and eye/hand coordination starts to develop.

Hearing

Children with normal hearing can hear as well as adults. Still you may notice your child responds more to sound once she reaches the age of 6 months. This is mainly because she is stronger and has greater control of her head and neck and can now turn towards sounds when she hears them. She starts making more distinct sounds and will also begin imitating simple sounds she hears. These are the beginning of her first words—she's practising language.

If you baby doesn't seem to respond to sound, and if she makes fewer noises instead of more, or if you're concerned about her hearing, ask a public health nurse or doctor for a referral to an audiologist for a hearing test. The earlier hearing problems are found, the earlier treatment can begin. Hearing can be tested at any age

Touch

Your baby explores by touch. As he starts to crawl, stand and walk, he will be able to discover and touch all kinds of things, both new and familiar. He is very curious and is unable to tell which new things are unsafe. He needs you to be near and to watch him at all times so he doesn't touch something that is harmful to himself or others.

Your baby begins to reach out for you with more purpose. He still needs and seeks the comfort of your touch, especially when he is feeling sick, hurt, frightened or tired.

Learning speech and language

From 6 to 18 months of age, babies start to use language. As she finds her voice, her babbling becomes words: from sounds such as *ooh, aah, babab* and *goo* to words such as *bye-bye, mama* and *doggie*.

As your baby understands more, she starts to copy gestures and point to things she recognizes. Enjoy your baby's delight and satisfaction in her new discoveries and abilities. It's exciting to see your baby learn and grow.

Children's first true words often occur when they're about 12 months old and are usually related to:

- Important people in their lives (*mama* or *dada*)
- Things that they interact with or things that move (*ball, kitty* or *cup*)

- Things they've done or felt (*run* or *hot*).

First words are often hard to understand by anyone other than moms and dads. For babies, learning words is a gradual process. In the beginning, your child may use one word to describe many things. For example, she may use *flower* to describe flowers, trees and bushes, not because she doesn't know that they are different, but because she doesn't have a word for all of them yet. She may also use one word for a whole thought. For instance, *shoe* may mean: "Those are my shoes," "I need my shoes," or "I don't want to wear my shoes."

Children copy single words they hear. Your baby should be able to say 10 to 20 single words by 18 months.

Learning more than one language

If you speak more than one language, use the one you are most comfortable with when talking to your baby. Speaking your first language at home creates a solid foundation for your child to learn both a first and second language. When you speak the language that you are most comfortable and familiar with, you'll speak and read more to your child.

Don't worry if others speak a different language to your baby. Babies can learn more than one language at a time. When your child is learning more than one language, remember that:

- Whatever the language, your baby needs to hear the words repeatedly before he tries to say them.
- Learning takes time. Your child may understand and say some words from all the languages he is learning.
- It is normal for him to use words from all the languages, even in the same sentence.
- Learning more than one language at a time does not slow down language development. Children who have difficulty learning words will likely have that same challenge in any language they learn.

What you can do: reading, talking and playing

To encourage your baby's learning and exploring, you can:

- Follow his lead. Your baby looks at and reaches for things he's interested in. Use words to describe what he's looking at or doing.
- Remember there is no right or wrong way to play. As long as an activity is safe, be interested in what your baby is interested in. Be ready to help if needed, but see what he does first. Babies learn through play and they love to do the same thing over and over.

Discovering something for the first time or for the 100th time fascinates your child.

- Watch for cues. Babies have short attention spans and too much play can be tiring and frustrating. When your baby looks away or no longer responds to an activity, it's time to do something else.

- Share books and sing songs. The rhythm and repetition of songs, stories and nursery rhymes encourage language and learning.

Playing and moving

Between 6 and 18 months, your baby learns to crawl and walk. She may even run, but may fall down often. Movement helps your baby explore and be a part of the world around her. When combined, play and movement encourage active living and a healthy lifestyle.

Give your baby lots of chances to move freely. Avoid keeping her in a baby carrier, stroller or car seat for long periods at a time. Use such equipment only as intended.

As much as possible, follow your child's lead and be a part of your child's playtimes.

What you can do: be active with your baby

- **Crawl.** As your baby learns to crawl, lead the way around different objects such as a chair or a box. Crawl through a hoop, cardboard box tunnel or tires in a playground. Crawl over and under objects, such as over cushions and under a table or another person's body.

- **Support.** Gently hold your baby from behind and under her upper arms as she learns to walk. Keep her hands free for balance.

- **Encourage.** Sit or stand in front of your child and encourage her to step toward you. Gradually increase the distance between you and your child as balance improves.

- **Mix it up.** Activities don't always have to be planned. Trips to the zoo or the park just because it is a nice day help your child learn there's always time for active play.

Play and toys

When your child is 6 to 18 months, you are his most important and most enjoyable playmate. Toys can be fun and can extend play, but aren't always needed. To your baby, you are the best toy in the room!

Toy-free activities you and your baby can enjoy include:
- Exploring the living room on your hands and knees
- Copying each other's expressions or movements
- Making a snowman, snow fort or snowballs
- Blowing bubbles—in the bath or in the backyard
- Playing hide-and-seek in the house or in a pile of autumn leaves
- Discovering a worm after a rainfall
- Going to the playground
- Singing and dancing.

When choosing toys, look for ones that allow your child to *do* rather than just *watch*. Make sure all toys are right for your baby's age. Toys that grow with a child, such as sturdy building blocks or a ball, are enjoyed for many years. Toys also need to stand up to being chewed, dropped, shaken, thrown, stepped on and washed. And, of course, make sure toys are safe. Toys with small or breakable parts can be dangerous for babies. (Also see *Safe and clean toys* on page 116).

Toys that interest babies at this age include:
- Music boxes
- Pictures of faces
- Soft, safe, chewable books
- Unbreakable mirrors
- Soft, cuddly toys
- Stacking rings or nesting blocks
- Plastic cups and containers
- Toy telephones
- Toys that make interesting sounds
- Rattles
- Easy-to-hold objects
- Large balls
- Trucks, cars
- Activity centres that turn, rattle and play music.

Feelings and emotions

6 to 12 months

Babies recognize and express a wider range of emotions than infants. This makes it easier for you to tell when your baby is happy, sad, mad or scared. Your baby now begins to read the emotions of other people too. She looks at your reactions in new and surprising situations to help figure out how she should respond. If you smile and look happy when someone visits, your baby finds it easier to accept that person.

Your baby's temperament also affects how she responds to new situations. (See a full description of temperament under *Getting along with others* on page 75). She starts to really know and love the people who care for her and you may find she starts to fuss more with strangers or change. Some babies find it more difficult than others to cope with new people and changes in routines.

Attachment, which is the sense of security your child gains from knowing you are there to offer comfort and safety, deepens and strengthens during this time. When you consistently give your baby loving care and safe surroundings, she learns to trust that you will take care of her. Your baby wants to watch you and be near you. Put her in a safe place where she can see and hear you while you are doing everyday activities like cooking and cleaning.

There will be times when you are in the middle of doing something and your child will need to wait for a minute for your attention. That is a normal part of every family's daily experience. When children are sick, hurt, scared or sad, however, they need their parents to provide comfort quickly and warmly.

At times, you may not be able to help your baby stop crying. What's important is to stay calm and gentle so she knows you care. Even if you are unable to soothe her, she knows you are there for her. See *Crying* on page 71.

12 to 18 months

From 12 to 18 months, your baby gets better at understanding the emotions of others. He learns that sometimes you are happy and sometimes you are unhappy with his behaviour. For the most part, children this age like to please.

Your baby's days are now a constant cycle of going out to explore and coming back to feel secure. These two forces are completely connected. When your baby feels safe and trusts you to protect him, he feels confident to go out and explore. Coming back to you is his way of sharing his discoveries and seeking comfort and security. It's as if he has emotional batteries that need constant recharging with a hug or a cuddle.

Finding a balance between these two opposite forces is a challenge for both children and parents. Your child needs to feel secure, so he stays close to you, but he also needs to explore, and increasingly wants to do things on his own.

Parents often feel torn between needing to protect their child and recognizing they must let their child do some things on his own.

Your baby gives you cues he needs comfort and security when he:

- Comes to you
- Needs a hug
- Follows you
- Wants to cuddle
- Looks for you
- Clings
- Reaches to be picked up.

Your baby gives you cues he wants and needs to explore when he:

- Rolls
- Puts things in his mouth
- Crawls
- Walks
- Runs
- Is curious about the world around him.

The way your child explores is based on his temperament. A child who doesn't like change may respond slowly to exploring new situations, while an active child may jump right in. Every child is different.

Safe and secure

You are your baby's secure home base from which he goes into the world. To build his self-confidence, he needs you to encourage safe exploration while providing the security of knowing you'll be there for him when he returns. When he runs back to you with his arms outstretched, he may want to be picked up, comforted, cuddled or just reassured. With time and experience, you will eventually find what's right (and comfortable) for both of you.

By 18 months, your baby is becoming a toddler and the limits you need to set may frustrate him. He doesn't yet understand the possible dangers he faces and that he needs to be watched all the time. His need to explore is far greater than his ability to stay safe.

Watch your child closely while he explores to help him avoid dangers. Make your home both childproof (make changes so your child cannot get into things that are dangerous), and child-friendly (put things that your child can have within easy reach or at his height; for example, books, toys and plastic cups). Moving or redirecting him works better than just telling him about dangers, which at this age, he can neither understand nor remember.

Your child learns best when you let him take the lead, let him explore in his own way and stay close enough to help if he needs you. Encourage your baby to explore without fear, and understand that you need to let him go to let him grow.

Dealing with powerful feelings

Your baby learns about feelings through her relationship with you. As she does she:

- Begins to recognize that she has her own feelings
- Often knows what she wants, but can't say it with words
- Finds it hard to understand another person's feelings or views
- Has very little self-control.

Feelings are very powerful for children, and as your baby becomes able to do more things on her own, her feelings may sometimes overwhelm her.

Babies don't have the language skills to express how they are feeling, so they often show their emotions with their body. You may see the first signs of temper tantrums as your baby approaches 18 months of age.

What you can do: helping your baby deal with feelings

- **Describe.** Name your baby's feelings—it's the first step in eventually understanding and controlling impulses and emotions.

- **Empathize.** Let her know you understand her frustration. For example, "I know you feel mad when you can't have the toy you want."

- **Distract.** Bring in another interesting toy, game or song.

- **Redirect.** Change the activity or move it to a more suitable place.

- **Reinforce.** Encourage positive behaviour by noticing it *and* commenting on it.

Temper tantrums

Babies are easily overwhelmed by their emotions. They are too young to understand or tell you how they feel, so they show it with their body. Meltdowns—or tantrums, hitting, biting and outbursts—become more common as babies become toddlers. Most children show some form of physical aggression by the time they are 17 months old.

Young children don't act out like this on purpose. These physical reactions are uncontrollable outbursts of fear, frustration, anger, tiredness or even hunger, and they are a cry for help.

Preventing these outbursts works much better than trying to get a child this age to understand or say what's wrong. See *Preventing tantrums* on page 140.

What you can do: taming a tantrum

How to help your child when he's overwhelmed:

- Give him space. Don't crowd him; make sure he's safe. Some children like to be held when they feel out of control.
- Stay with him. Remain quiet and calm with him until he's calmer.
- Talk about it. After he has settled down, talk quietly about his feelings. Help him give his feelings a name—it is the first step to understanding them.
- Give simple directions. Let your child know: "We don't bite people. It hurts."
- Let him start over. Sometimes a child needs a second chance.
- Reinforce the positive. When you see positive behaviour, comment on it. "That's a very gentle way to pat the puppy."
- Understand. Try to understand why your child has had a tantrum; for example, is he hungry, angry, lonely, tired or sick? See *Temper tantrums* on page 139.
- Forget fault. A baby doesn't know why he has reacted the way he has, so he can't explain or apologize for his actions.
- Time with you, not time out. Time outs (see page 166) are not appropriate for babies. Time with you is the best way to teach your baby how to get along with others.

If you are consistent with your approach, your child learns that tantrums are not a way of getting his needs met and his tantrums will eventually decrease.

Your baby's world

Your baby's world is growing—and he is starting to explore what's around him. He now sees other people and things are separate from him, and wants to move toward them, or have them come to him. His new discoveries are big, bold and exciting; the curious nature of babies demands parents give them a watchful eye, hands-on attention, supportive care and safe surroundings.

Getting along with others

The second six months of a baby's life can be described as happy and sociable and your baby's most important playmate is you! Your baby enjoys playing simple games with you, copying your actions and delighting in your positive responses. She also enjoys listening to music and looking in mirrors. At this age, she thinks the reflection is another baby.

By 12 months, your baby begins to relate to more and more people. Play is important to all parts of your child's development. On a social level, when your child plays near and with other people, she learns how to get along with them. Once she starts walking, her world gets bigger and she needs to start being around other young children.

While your baby will enjoy and benefit from being around other children, you need to watch her closely. Her brain has not yet developed enough to let her learn how to share or cooperate. She could bite or hit new friends as easily as she greets or hugs them. She is curious and may just be exploring the only way she knows.

Your child may find it hard to get along with other children at first. No child learns how to get along with others or behave by just being told what to do. They learn with time, practice and their parents' gentle guidance. Children under 2 are not yet able to follow rules, but they need you to set limits so they can begin learning that rules exist.

You need to be very understanding and patient as your child learns to deal with limits, feelings and emotions. Be consistent. Babies must experience things many times before fully understanding how to act with people.

What you can do: as baby grows

- **Encourage.** Your encouragement is a powerful motivator and shows your baby you recognize that she is working hard to make new discoveries.

- **Stay close.** Your baby still needs to be held close, cuddled and sometimes carried. Be at your baby's level when she is playing with others so you can react quickly if needed.

- **Form routines.** Regular routines for feeding, bathing, playing and sleeping help your baby learn what to expect. They also give her comfort and security.

- **Be flexible.** As your child gets older, bend routines occasionally. It's good for your family and better for your child than a rigid schedule.

Separation anxiety

As early as 7 months old, but as late as 18 months, babies can develop separation anxiety. They become anxious when separated from their parents, especially their mothers. This feeling comes from a fear of being abandoned and can happen at bedtime (see *Sleeping* on page 100) or when parents leave their children with other caregivers (see *What you can do: starting childcare* on page 25). You can help your baby overcome this anxiety by building his feeling of security.

If your child gets anxious when you leave him with others during the day, try a series of short separations. Increase the amount of time you are away from him each time. If you can, arrange to take your baby to a friend's or relative's home for a short visit. Take his favourite toy or blanket for security. Spend some time with him so he's comfortable with his surroundings. Tell him you are going to leave and that you will be back soon. Say a quick goodbye before you leave with a hug and a wave.

Leave for a short time and give him a brief warm greeting when you return. Try these separations at regular intervals to help him recognize that other adults are not a threat and, most importantly, that you will always return.

While this may reduce the anxiety your child feels when away from you, time spent with you continues to be central to his sense of security.

Protecting your baby

Once mobile, babies want to go everywhere and do everything. As they learn and explore, they also place things in their mouths and try new things to test their limits. Their minds and bodies, however, cannot always keep up to their keen sense of discovery. They have no idea their travels can put them at risk of an injury.

Babies do not deliberately try to get into trouble. They are just curious and trying to discover the world around them. Young children cannot respect danger until they understand it. This won't happen until they are much older.

You may know what hot is, but your baby does not. She has no idea that a cup of hot coffee could result in a bad scald or burn. In the same way, your baby doesn't know that climbing up something is often easier than climbing back down.

Help your baby's spirit of discovery thrive while still keeping her safe. Understand and anticipate her development and create safe places for her to live in and explore.

What you can do: create a safer environment

- **Play safe.** Babies need constant and active supervision during their waking hours, whether indoors or outdoors. Active supervision means knowing your child's abilities, closely watching her, and being nearby to quickly direct her to a safer activity if she gets into a risky situation. Babies are too young to be left alone inside or out.

- **Water safe.** Always stay with your young child when she is in or near a bathtub or any body of water. Children can drown in seconds in less than 25 mm (1 inch) of water. Baby bath seats, life jackets, water wings and other devices are not a safe substitute for adult supervision.

- **Lock-up.** Keep dangerous items, such as cleaning solutions, matches, cosmetics and medications, in locked cupboards out of your baby's reach. Remove poisonous plants indoors and out. Call the Alberta Poison Centre immediately at 403-944-1414 if you think your child has been poisoned.

- **Child proof and child-friendly.** Put treasured keepsakes away for a few months or put up a gate so your baby can't go in a certain room. Remove or modify furniture with sharp edges. Choose and arrange child-friendly areas in your house.

- **Furniture.** Secure heavy furniture like bookcases and dressers to the wall before your child begins to climb on things. Move furniture away from windows and install window safety latches to avoid falls.

- **Cribs.** Move the crib mattress to its lowest position once your child can pull up to a standing position to help prevent falls. Before your child is able to climb over the crib rails, move her to a toddler bed.

- **Gates.** Install safety gates at the top and bottom of stairs. Use wall-mounted gates at the top; pressure gates can fall over under your child's weight.

- **Gear.** Wear and use safety gear properly. Make sure you use the right safety equipment for your child when it's needed, for example, bike helmets when in a bike trailer, child safety seats in cars, restraining straps in strollers and high chairs. Children learn much more from what we *do* than what we *say*. When you wear a seatbelt or bike helmet, you are a powerful role model.

- **Bugs, weather and sun.** Have fun and stay healthy outside. See *The great outdoors* on page 30 on protecting your child from the elements.

Travel safely

Match your child's car seat to his size and age:
- Use a **rear-facing seat** until your child is at least 1 year old *and* weighs 9 kg (20 lbs.).
- Then, use a **forward-facing car seat** appropriate for your child's height and weight until your child is at least 18 kg (40 lbs.).

Know how to install and use your baby's car seat:
- First, consult the instructions that come with your child's safety seat and the instructions in your vehicle owner's manual.

- Next, take the appropriate Child Safety Seat Yes Test (available in your copy of *From Here Through Maternity*, from your community health centre or at www.albertahealthservices.ca)
- Call Health Link Alberta for information on car seat classes offered in your community or if you have other questions.

Safe and clean toys

If something goes into your baby's hands, you can expect it to go into your baby's mouth. If it can fit through a toilet paper roll, it is too small for a baby or young child. Choose only toys right for your baby's age.

Tasting and chewing are natural ways for babies to explore. Durable and washable toys are a good choice for your baby. To clean toys, wash them in hot soapy water, rinse and air dry. Cloth or washable stuffed toys can be cleaned in a washing machine and dried in a hot dryer. Durable plastic toys can be cleaned in your dishwasher. Cleaning toys is especially important when your child is sick as it reduces re-infection and the spread of germs.

Stay healthy

Regular health checkups (at the doctor, dentist and optometrist) and routine vaccinations help keep babies healthy. To find out if your baby's vaccinations are up to date, call your local community health centre. For more suggestions on keeping children safe and healthy at every age, see *Protecting your child* on page 26 and *Keeping your child healthy* on page 32.

Caring for you

Now that you are a parent, you may find friends without children less than eager to hear about your child's first taste of pureed carrots and that you've lost interest in a night on the town or the latest workplace gossip. You might even find yourself turning down a chance to see old friends because your interests have changed.

For all its rewards, becoming a parent brings big changes to your life. Some parents can feel isolated and lonely. This is true for both moms and dads, whether you are at home full time or in the paid workforce.

It's important to your well-being to connect with other adults and parents (with or without your baby). It gives you a chance to get out of the house, go somewhere other than just to work and share both personal and parenting joys and challenges.

Babies

What you can do: connecting with others

- **Reach out.** Start with family members, they're most likely to be interested and supportive. Neighbours and friends are good choices too, especially those who have children.

- **Sign up.** Alberta Health Services and many community agencies have groups for both moms and dads and their new babies. These programs are a great way to get out and meet other new parents and get more parenting information. Call Health Link Alberta for details.

- **Go online.** Many online chat rooms, discussion forums and blogs are dedicated to parenting. All have advice, so be a critical thinker—compare information you get online to a source you can trust (like *From Here Through Maternity* and *Growing Miracles*, which are written by experts on child development and health). If you have questions, talk to your public health nurse, doctor or call Health Link Alberta.

- **Check it out.** Many libraries offer family storytime programs for children of all ages. Your child is never too young to enjoy these.

- **Stay awhile.** Next time you visit your local park or coffee shop, stay and have a chat, with other parents or patrons.

- **Get out.** Join a walking or running club, or call a friend and start your own.

- **Keep in touch.** Many parents who have attended prenatal or early parenting classes continue the friendships they've formed by getting together long after the classes are done.

- **Go together.** Local sports and fitness clubs and facilities offer a variety of mom and tot, or dad and tot programs. Childcare is often available. Check with your local church, community centre, family resource centre, and family service agencies about programs offered for parents and children, or parents alone, for example, parenting groups, drop-in programs, Parent Link Centres, etc.

- **Get more information.** Call 211, or go to www.informalberta.ca for information about programs and services in your community.

Toddlers
18 MONTHS TO 3 YEARS

*You know children are growing up when they start
asking questions that have answers.*

—John J. Plomp

Growing with your toddler

Toddlers come by their name because they toddle—walk and move—with growing confidence and skill. They are bundles of energy, excitement and emotion in constant motion.

Toddlers' brains develop rapidly. As toddlers realize they are separate people from their parents, they want and need to test their thoughts and everything around them. Toddlers need their parents to set limits, since what they want to do and what they can actually do are not always the same.

As the parent of a toddler, you need to set reasonable, but firm limits for your child. It's normal and necessary for your toddler to test those limits in order for him to grow and learn. When he realizes your boundaries are firm, he is likely to have bursts of emotion such as frustration and temper tantrums.

Such outbursts are normal and with your help, your child will learn how to deal with these emotions. For toddlers, it's all part of growing up and getting to know themselves.

At times, toddlers may seem like little adults, but their minds and bodies are still growing and being shaped. They must continually explore and experience everything around them before they can truly understand who they are and how to behave.

The toddler years are often called the *terrible twos* because dealing with toddlers' constant energy and emotion can be very demanding. When parents stop to appreciate their child's eagerness to learn and excitement in sharing new discoveries they realize this stage can be just as easily thought of as *terrific toddlers*.

Your toddler's body

As babies become toddlers, their growth tends to slow, their body shape evens out and they move faster and more often. They like to do things on their own, but they still need reassurance and security from their parents. Knowing a parent or adult is watching over them gives toddlers the comfort and confidence to go out into the world.

Toddlers are very physical beings and from the moment they take their first steps, they want to go faster, climb higher and move in new ways. They quickly learn to run, jump, back up, turn around, kick, squat, climb and bounce. Sometimes they move to the rhythm of music and sometimes they move to the beat of their own drum. Watching them can be entertaining, tiring and nerve-wracking all at once. By encouraging safe physical activity at this age, you can help your child remain active for a lifetime. If you are physically active, your child is more likely to be active, too.

At first, your toddler may need your help and encouragement to try new activities; coordination comes with practice. She needs to hold your hand when going up and down stairs, but also needs the chance to run free in a playground or gym. She is able to climb up and over things (like furniture and playground equipment), but may have trouble getting down. She can throw a small ball overhand, but it won't always go where she wants. Your toddler needs lots of chances to exercise her big muscles. A walk in the park, an afternoon at the playground and an hour making a snowman all give your toddler a chance to develop, be active, have fun and be with you.

Not all physical motion in toddlers is big and fast. Toddlers also practise smaller movements such as turning doorknobs, keys and screws or undoing large buttons or zippers on clothes. They build bigger towers from blocks (at least six blocks high), push or pull a toy while walking and scribble or draw pictures.

Between the ages of 18 months and 5 years, children gain about 1.4 to 2.3 kg (3 to 5 lbs.) a year and grow about 6 cm (2-1/2 in.) a year. They begin to look more like a young child than a baby as their legs, arms and body grow more in proportion to their head.

Toddlers soon realize boys and girls are different. Your toddler may be very curious about her own and other people's bodies. Learning where urine (pee) and bowel movements (poop) come from helps her get ready for toilet teaching.

Your family may have names for the body parts that make boys and girls different, but as part of healthy sexual development, toddlers should also know their correct names: penis, testicles, breasts, vulva and vagina.

Eating

Typical toddlers

While not every toddler has them, feeding challenges are common with toddlers. From picky eating to food jags, dawdling to changing appetites, it is hard for parents to know what to expect from one day to the next or how to deal with these typical behaviours so they don't become power struggles.

Common food challenges for toddlers include:

- **Rigid preferences.** Toddlers may only want to try new foods when it's their idea. Their likes and dislikes change all the time; what they like one day, they may say they hate the next. Many toddlers like to touch and smell food, but not taste it; this is a normal way of exploring and learning about food.
- **Food jags.** Toddlers like what they like! When your child asks for the same food over and over, it's called a food jag. This normal behaviour eventually passes.
- **Slow eating.** Toddlers can dawdle over food. It can take them 20 to 30 minutes to finish their meal. Toddlers are interested in (and distracted by) everything around them and may find it hard to focus on eating.
- **Changing appetite.** Healthy toddlers eat when they are hungry. As the rapid growth rate of the baby years levels off, appetites naturally adjust and parents may see this change as poor eating. If your child is healthy, growing and developing, he's likely getting enough to eat.
- **Messy meals.** Toddlers like to eat with their hands, but can also learn to use a fork and a spoon. They can usually drink well from a cup but may have difficulty putting the cup down. Mealtimes are still messy.

The importance of milk

Some mothers and toddlers choose to continue breastfeeding. This healthy choice is supported by Health Canada and the World Health Organization; both recommend breastfeeding until the age of 2 years and beyond.

Whole-fat cow's milk (homogenized or 3.25% milk fat) is an excellent source of nutrition for young toddlers. It has a higher fat content than 2%, 1% or skim milk, and is a better source of energy and many of the nutrients toddlers' bodies and brains need to grow and develop. You can switch to lower-fat milk after your child is 2 years old. Milk is low in iron so you need to give your toddler a variety of iron-rich foods to meet her needs.

As your toddler eats more solid foods, she may drink less milk. Milk is still an important part of her diet and she needs 500 to 750 ml (2 to 3 cups) a day.

Quenching thirst

Offer water anytime. Offer juice or milk only with meals and snacks. Sugar-sweetened drinks have no nutritional value. When sipped throughout the day, they increase the risk of cavities and can make your child too full to eat healthier foods. Limit juice to 125 ml ($1/2$ cup) a day; use only 100% unsweetened, pasteurized juice, serve it in a cup and only with meals or planned snacks.

The feeding relationship

As a parent, don't feel you have to run a 24-hour diner that caters only to your child's tastes. Children need to be offered a variety of foods so they eventually try them.

For toddlers and their parents, the feeding relationship becomes even more important. Parents are responsible for *what* they give their child to eat and *when* and *where* they give meals and snacks. A toddler is responsible for choosing *whether* to eat and *how much*.

In a healthy feeding relationship, children learn to eat well and mealtimes are less challenging. Children also learn to make healthy food choices on their own.

You cannot make a child eat and a determined toddler can usually out-wait even the most patient parent. If your child refuses to eat a meal but is hungry 20 minutes later, you can either re-offer him something from his meal (such as some fruit or cheese) or kindly and firmly remind him that he must wait until the next planned snack.

Encourage your toddler to try new food, but let him decide to go beyond one bite—do not force him to eat. You may have to offer some foods 15 times or more before your child is comfortable with them. Offering a healthy food you know your child likes at each meal helps make mealtimes more successful.

How much your toddler eats depends on your toddler—and it can change daily. Toddlers eat less than adults, and children know when they are full. If forced to eat past that point, they learn to ignore their body's fullness signals.

For more information, ask your public health nurse for a copy of *Food Guide Serving Sizes for 1-5 Years*.

What you can do: your role in the feeding relationship

What food to give

- Choose a variety of foods from the four main food groups of Canada's Food Guide.
- Offer a variety of textures.
- Limit milk products with high sugar content, such as chocolate milk, milkshakes, sweetened yogurt, frozen yogurt, ice cream, custard and eggnog. Also, limit processed cheese, which is high in salt.
- Offer healthy meals and snacks—your child will come to expect them.
- Be a role model. Toddlers want to eat what they see others eating. You may need to cut up some foods so they don't pose a choking risk (for example, grapes, apples and carrots, etc). See *Foods to avoid* on page 29.

When to eat

- Provide a regular supply of energy throughout the day. Three meals and three planned snacks a day help your toddler grow and develop.
- Try to keep to your toddler's schedule, even if you have to change yours. Hungry toddlers are cranky toddlers.
- If you are out on errands, take a healthy, portable snack with you.

Where to eat

- Teach your toddler to sit to eat so she doesn't choke and she learns to pay attention to eating.
- A meal around a table lets your whole family share the day's events and connect with each other. This builds the strong family relationships that are important to healthy child development.
- Turn off the TV. People who eat in front of the TV are more likely to overeat as they ignore the signals that say, "I'm full."

If you are concerned about your child's eating, talk to your public health nurse or call Health Link Alberta.

Teeth and oral health

Toddlers have all their baby teeth by the age of 2 or 3 years and while they may want to brush their own teeth, they are still too young to do a good job. Let your child try, then help finish the job. You will need to help him with brushing and flossing until he is about 8 years old. When he can *write* his own name (around Grade 3), he has the skills to be able to brush properly.

How to brush

- Use water only (no toothpaste) until your child is at least 3 years old and able to spit. Talk to your dentist before using fluoridated products with your child.
- Hold the bristles of the toothbrush at a slant against the gumline and move back and forth gently with very short strokes or circles.
- Count to 10 while brushing in one area. Move to the next area and repeat.
- Brush the outside surfaces of the teeth, the inside surfaces and then the tops (chewing surfaces).
- Gently brush the tongue from back to front.
- Floss teeth daily (see *Using dental floss* on page 99)

What you can do: brushing your child's teeth

- Find a position that works best for you and your child, such as sitting on a chair, stool or even the side of the bathtub. If you are behind or beside your child, it is easier to see into his mouth. This position is generally more comfortable for you and your child.
- Support your child's head against your leg or with your hand or free arm.
- Set a timer or play or sing a favourite song so your child learns how long it takes to do a thorough job— about two minutes.
- Explain the importance of healthy teeth and gums and why it is important to learn to look after them.
- Set a good example. Let your child see you brushing and flossing. She wants to imitate you.

Regular dental exams

By 2 years of age, your child should have visited a dentist at least once. Regular dental visits can prevent or find tooth problems early, when simple steps can be taken to stop or repair any damage. These visits also help your child learn about and get comfortable with dental care. If you are unable to afford dental care, see *Alberta Child Health Benefit Plan* on page 35.

Dental emergencies

Injuries and infections of the gums or teeth are dental emergencies. Children are especially prone to broken teeth—80 per cent of broken teeth happen in childhood, usually when children are 2 to 4 years old and 8 to 10 years old. Ask your dentist about emergency services.

Sleeping

A pleasant, predictable bedtime routine helps your young toddler—and you—rest well night after night. Wind down your days with quiet time after supper, followed by a bath, brushing teeth and a bedtime song or story. Routines comfort children and make bedtime easier for them.

When you and your partner take turns putting your child to bed, your toddler learns the routine is the same even when the person changes. This also makes it much easier for a family member, friend or babysitter to put your child to sleep if you're out. If you're a single parent, you may want to have a relative or close friend give you a break once in a while.

By leaving the room before your child falls asleep, you let your child know that you are confident he can settle himself. Be matter-of-fact, and speak with a calm and friendly tone. Say goodnight, give him a kiss and leave the room. Toddlers are often afraid of being separated from their parents. Let your child know where you will be and that you will see him in the morning. A nightlight may help.

Your toddler may not fall asleep right away, but will drift off when he needs to. As he settles, he may talk, sing or play quietly in his crib. All are ways of self-soothing and having a little quiet time before sleeping. Your child may find extra comfort and security from objects, such as a special blanket or a cuddly stuffed toy, but keep his crib free of toys and objects he can climb on. A fall from a crib can seriously injure a toddler.

You can tell if your toddler is sleeping enough by the way he acts during the day. If he falls asleep outside regular nap time or is cranky, he may need more sleep at night. At this age, most children sleep about 11 to 12 hours a night.

Naps

Naps help your growing toddler make it through her busy days. Older babies and younger toddlers usually stop morning naps between the ages of 1 and 2 years. By 2 years of age, most children have a one- to two-hour nap after lunch and may continue to nap until they're 3 to 6 years old. If your child naps for more than two hours at a time, she may have trouble sleeping at night.

Night terrors and nightmares

Some children experience periods of screaming and shaking during their sleep at night. Their eyes are open and they appear to be awake, but they aren't. This is called a *night terror* (or sleep terror). Night terrors usually happen in the first part of the night, about one to four hours after falling asleep, in the deepest part of the sleep cycle. They often occur at the same time each night and usually only last a few minutes before a child settles back to sleep.

During a night terror, a child may not be aware of anyone around him and seldom remembers the incident. For this reason, night terrors are much more upsetting to parents than to children.

Trying to physically comfort (hold or hug) a child having a night terror can make it last longer. Make sure your child is safe and don't try to wake him. If your child is having night terrors at the same time each night, you can try waking him 10 to 15 minutes before that time. Doing this for a few weeks can break the cycle. Night terrors are more common in boys and usually peak around the age of 2.

Nightmares are different. They are frightening dreams that a child can describe. Your child can wake up from a nightmare and if he does, he needs immediate physical comfort and reassurance. Nightmares usually happen in the second half of the night and your child might have trouble falling back to sleep.

Everyone has four or five dreams a night and occasional nightmares are normal. If your child's dreams are frequent and scary, try to find out if something is causing them. This could include something that has scared or hurt him, or a major change such as getting used to childcare, a new home or the arrival of a new baby. Talk to you doctor if your child's night fears are frequent or disrupting your family life.

From crib to bed

Going from a crib to a bed is a major step for toddlers and parents alike. Some children find the size of a bed overwhelming. Some parents are overwhelmed by how fast their child is growing up. Your toddler is ready to sleep in a bed when she tries to climb out of her crib. Moving her before she can climb out prevents falls.

Your nightly bedtime routine can help your child adjust to a bed. The routine may change a little—for example, you may change from reading a book in a rocker to reading a book in bed—but it remains important and largely the same. For the first few nights, your child may need an extra story, song or snuggle.

What you can do: helping your toddler into a bed

- Talk to your child about how big he's getting and all the new things he can do.
- Consider using a toddler bed (a smaller bed often fitted with a crib mattress).
- If space allows, set the bed up for naps and continue to use the crib at night.
- Use a side railing or put the mattress on the floor to keep your child from falling.
- Play soft music or use a nightlight to help your child quiet down before falling asleep.
- Offer your child a favourite toy or blanket; children this age often find comfort and security from them.

Bedroom safety

Before moving your toddler from a crib to a bed, make sure her room is safe and child-friendly:

- Use childproof covers on all electrical outlets.
- Check all furniture and furnishings. They should be stable and secure since toddlers love to climb and explore. Anything that can be pulled over, such as hanging pictures or bookshelves, should be bolted to the walls. Dresser drawers should be locked or have childproof latches (toddlers like to pull out drawers and climb up the frame).
- Blind, drapery and curtain cords should be short, secured and/or well out of reach.
- Do not put your child's bed under a window. Falling from an open window can seriously injure or kill a child. Window screens are meant to keep bugs out, not children in. They can give way under your child's weight. Window safety latches are advised, as long as an adult can quickly open them in an emergency.
- Remove any toys or objects that cause choking.
- Do not give your child a bottle or sippy cup in bed.

- Check the change table. Diapers, lotions, cream and wipes should be stored in a cupboard with a childproof latch or in another room. See What you can do: *Keep it clean* on page 76.

Bedtime resistance

Your child can learn that once he's in bed, he needs to stay there. He may want to get out for a number of reasons: he's more independent, he wants more control of his life, he's adjusting to a big bed or he's anxious about being away from you. He may beg to stay up, refuse to lie down or even have a temper tantrum.

What you can do: peaceful bedtimes

- Follow a bedtime routine that works for your family.
- If your child comes out of her bedroom once you have put her to bed, take her by the hand, lead her back to her room and tuck her in. Stay calm and matter-of-fact; don't argue.
- Avoid saying anything other than: "It's time for bed." By being kind, you let her know you appreciate her struggle. By being firm, you let her know that bedtime is bedtime. You may have to do this several times for several nights, but eventually your child will learn that you mean what you say. The key to success is staying calm (deep breathing helps!).
- Close, don't lock her door. Most fire departments recommend closing all bedroom doors at night to protect your family from fire and smoke but locking your child's bedroom door can frighten her and can be dangerous. If your child is frightened with the door closed, you can use a baby gate in the doorway to keep your toddler from wandering out. Once she has gone to sleep, take the gate down and shut the door for the night.

Toddlers and toilets

Learning to use a toilet can't be rushed. It's important to wait until your child is both physically ready (muscles that control the bowel and bladder have to be strong enough) and motivated to learn. This way toilet teaching takes less time and is less frustrating and disappointing for you and your toddler.

Most children are at least 2-1/2 years old before they are physically ready to learn how to use the toilet. Even then, they also need to be interested. Give yourself and your child lots of time and avoid deadlines.

Your toddler may be ready for this important developmental step if he:

- Stays dry for several hours or through the night
- Has bowel movements at fairly predictable times
- Is aware he is urinating or having a bowel movement
- Can pull down loose-fitting pants and follow simple directions
- Doesn't like to be in wet or soiled diapers
- Can tell you he needs to use the toilet
- Shows interest in using the potty or in other people using the toilet.

Start slowly

Time and patience are the keys to toilet teaching. Begin by helping your toddler recognize when she is *going*. Talk to her, using words that are familiar to your family.

Let your toddler see you use the toilet. When you have to go to the bathroom, interrupt your activities and let her know where you're going. You can also let her see you emptying the contents of her soiled diapers into the toilet and then flushing so she can understand where bowel movements should go. These things help her develop the thinking process she needs to learn to use the toilet.

Set up a potty chair in the bathroom and explain what it's for. Let her approach it on her own time. Reading books about toilet teaching is another way to get your child used to using the toilet. Local libraries carry a good selection of children's books on toilet teaching and other toddler-related subjects.

Simple steps

Learning to use the toilet is a complex task for children. Breaking the task into simple steps helps your child learn over a period of days or weeks.

- Begin by showing your child his potty and explaining how it's used. Let him know you'll help him.
- Ask your child to tell you when he needs to go to the toilet. Watch for signs he's about to go. These include: stopping what he's doing, looking down or off in the distance or saying: "Oh, oh." He may also fidget or hold his hand between his legs. If you ask him if he has to go, he is likely to say, "No!" If you say, "Looks like you have to go to the bathroom," or "Let's get you to the bathroom," you may get faster action. Your toddler probably won't be able to wait more than a few moments.

- Stay with your child while he's on the toilet.
- Little boys want to pee standing up like their dad or other boys and men. It might be easier for them to learn by sitting first, and then switch to standing when they know what to do.
- Encourage your child's efforts, successful or otherwise. Get him into the habit of washing his hands whenever he's been in the bathroom.
- If after a couple of weeks your child is not making progress, he is likely not ready to learn. Stop and try again in a few weeks or when he seems more interested.

Take a seat

Your toilet's seat may be too big—or too scary—for your toddler. A training potty that sits on the floor, or a toilet seat adapter that fits on your toilet, can make your toddler feel safer and more comfortable.

If you use a potty

- Make sure it's sturdy and doesn't tip easily.
- Your child may feel safer because her feet are on the floor and she won't be afraid of falling in.
- Your child will quickly be able to get on and off without your help.
- Your child is able to see the *results*.

If you use a toilet-seat adapter

- It should fit securely, otherwise it may pinch or your child may be afraid of falling.
- Your child may be scared if the toilet is flushed while she's sitting on it. Many children this age fear being flushed down the toilet or being sucked down the bathtub drain. Let her know she is too big for this to happen. Respect her fear by letting her flush the toilet once she is off.
- Use a step stool so your child can get on and off easily. To feel stable and secure, your child's feet should touch the stool when seated.

What you can do: set the stage for success

- Take your child to the toilet after waking (in the morning or after naps), before going out and before a bath.
- Keep the potty in a bathroom close to where your toddler spends most of the day.
- Keep books in the bathroom to help your child sit longer.
- Keep the potty clean so your child wants to use it.
- Dress your toddler in clothes that are easy to pull up and down.
- The sound of running water may help the urge to pee.
- Be consistent. You and other caregivers need to have the same approach and expectations for your child to learn to use the toilet.
- Be patient, positive and relaxed. Don't set deadlines. Children learn in their own way and on their own time.

Oops!

Expect setbacks—it takes time to learn this new skill. Toileting accidents are not something children do on purpose. Some children may begin to have more accidents if family life changes because of:

- A new baby
- Interrupted routines
- New or different childcare
- Stress in the family
- Illness or injury.

Your child may feel bad about these lapses. Reassure him that this is part of learning and that he's loved and supported. A calm, matter-of-fact approach helps him get back on track.

Dressing and undressing

As your little one becomes an older toddler, she will dress and undress with more skill. She may not be able to get in and out of her clothes as quickly as when you help, but a toddler needs to have the chance to learn what she can do on her own. You may need to help her dress on mornings when everyone is rushed, but on other days, let her dress herself at her own pace.

Clothes with elastic waists and Velcro are easier for toddlers to get on and off. Shoes and boots that slip on or do up with Velcro are easier to manage for young children. Most children aren't able to tie their own shoes until they are 5 or 6 years old.

Toddlers like to make their own choices and you may find your toddler picks the same clothes day after day. You can help her choose clothes based on the day's plans and activities. Divide her clothes into *special occasion* and *play* clothes. Let her choose from the clothes suited to the occasion. Choices make children feel grown-up and independent. You may think plaid pants and polka dot T-shirts don't match, but your toddler is proud of her choice.

Your toddler's mind

Children 18 months to 3 years old do so much more than toddle. Their minds are as busy as their bodies as they learn to use words and discover new kinds of play. It is no wonder many parents find this stage of childhood exhausting. It's easier to help your toddler when you understand all the things she's going through.

Toddlers are just learning who they are and they define themselves by what belongs to them. They have a powerful sense of what is theirs! Being able to walk and move helps them realize that they are separate beings from their moms and dads. Suddenly, they can do all kinds of new things and this can be exciting for them. It can also lead to anxiety when they realize they can be left alone.

Toddlers often want to do more than they can. Their brains are developing and their language skills are growing, but they still can't always say what they need. This can lead to frustration. "No!" is the best way they have to tell you that they want to do things by themselves.

As well, toddlers are very impulsive. This means they act without thinking, because their brain is still developing. To learn about their world, they need to explore, and this need is as strong as their need to eat and sleep.

Rules are something toddlers are unable to understand or follow. They learn over time that rules exist. When you set limits on what your toddler can and cannot do, you are helping her learn to follow rules, but this takes lots of patience and repetition.

Toddlers are very physical beings. Their first instinct is to throw their bodies into their responses, whether hitting someone in frustration or wrapping themselves around a loved one for a hug.

From now and until they are early preschoolers, children see themselves as the centre of the universe. This is not selfish; it is completely normal, and a necessary stage of development. They are unable to see things from any point of view than their own, therefore, they cannot feel sorry or ashamed. As their experience grows and their brains develops further, toddlers recognize other people also have feelings. The more complex feelings and shame or jealousy come later.

Knowing these things are typical of all toddlers can help you better understand your child's behaviour. Take good care of yourself. It takes lots of energy and patience to parent toddlers.

Exploring through the senses

Your toddler continues to explore through his senses. Seeing, hearing, tasting, touching and smelling are all ways to learn about the world around him. You can help build the brain connections he needs for learning when you encourage him to use his senses whenever it is safe to do so. When you think of learning this way, you'll find hundreds of ways to turn everyday activities into learning adventures.

Talk to your doctor or public health nurse if you are concerned about your child's vision, hearing or interactions with you and others. Your toddler's vision should be checked by age 3 and again at 6 years old. See *Vision* on page 162 for the signs of vision problems.

Learning speech and language

Toddlers rapidly learn new words and begin using them in two-word sentences such as: "More cracker" or "Mommy, shoe."

At all once your child tells you so much more. She lets you know she doesn't like something by shaking her head and saying, "No," or "Not." She asks questions by using words such as, "Where?" and, "What's that?" Her understanding of words takes a dramatic leap, and she is able to answer simple questions such as, "Do you want a drink of water?" or, "Where's your blanket?" She is also able to follow simple directions like, "Bring Daddy your shoes."

Between the ages of 2 and 3, toddlers' sentences get longer (four to five words or more) and more grammatically correct. Your toddler begins using plurals, articles (*the, a* and *an*) and pronouns (*she, he, you* and *I*), although not always correctly at first. You and your toddler begin having short conversations about things that interest her.

Language is still new to your toddler and you may not always understand everything she says. Continue helping your toddler learn language skills by letting her experience language in different ways (songs, poems and conversations with other people), reading to her every day and playing with her.

Talk by 2, understand me by 3

Even a quiet child eagerly uses new language skills.

By 18 months old, children can usually:
- Say 10 to 20 words
- Point to three body parts such as nose, toes and tummy
- Follow simple instructions such as, "Get your ball."
- Be understood by others about 25 per cent of the time.

By 2 years old, children can usually:
- Say more than 20 words
- Use two-word sentences such as, "More milk."
- Follow longer directions such as, "Get the ball and throw it to Mommy."
- Be understood 50 to 75 per cent of the time.

By 3 years old, children can usually:
- Say a word for almost everything
- Use two- to three-word sentences such as, "That my truck."
- Answer simple questions such as, "What's your name?"
- Be understood 75 to 100 per cent of the time.

If you are concerned about your child's speech, help is available. Acting early on your concerns is important. In Alberta, speech-language pathology services are free and parents do not need a doctor's referral. For more information, call Health Link Alberta.

Play and playing

Toddlers

Being active

Children love to be physically active. Unfortunately, safety concerns, TV, video games and demanding schedules are modern realities that have decreased children's level of activity. Your child needs you to provide daily opportunities and encouragement to make active living a lifelong habit.

Movement is important to your child's developing body and mind. It helps improve fine and gross motor skills and helps release tension and energy. When you move with your toddler, he gets a chance to have fun and spend time with you.

Movement is also the foundation of many activities that can be shared with other people, such as play, exploration, sport, dance, drama and crafts. In fact, movement is part of everyday life. From walking to school with a group of friends to shovelling snow for a neighbour, active living teaches children how to get along with others.

To keep your child physically active, both now and throughout his life:
- Make it fun.
- Start now. Your child is never too young to be active.
- Begin simply. Running, jumping, kicking, throwing and catching are the building blocks for tasks and activities requiring more complex movements.
- Plan activities that match the seasons, your child's abilities and your family's interests and resources.
- Encourage effort—it fosters your child's self-esteem.
- Play along. Play is good for adults too.
- Don't overdo it. Balance activity and rest, and pause often for water.
- Try to go outside every day as the weather allows. The fresh air and change of surroundings are good for everyone.

Pretend-play

Toddlers learn about life and develop their imagination through the wonderful world of pretend-play.

Young children pretend by acting out real-life situations. They pretend to take a nap, feed their stuffed animals or give their doll a bath. At first, they use props that look like the real thing (for example, a toy broom can only be a broom). Before long their pretend-play becomes more advanced. Now objects can be anything they can imagine: a piece of cardboard becomes a flying carpet, a chopstick can be a magic wand and a broom can be a galloping pony!

You may notice your toddler talking to herself as she plays. This is how children start to organize their thinking. This *out-loud* thinking eventually becomes what is called *inner speech*—something all adults have. The ability to talk things through is very helpful for children as they learn to solve problems and deal with emotions. As their talking skills improve, toddlers start to include other children and adults in their pretend-play.

When your toddler pretends, she is learning concepts that will help her read, write, think, solve problems, and get along with others. To her it's just fun—and so it should be.

What you can do: encouraging pretend-play

- **Follow your toddler's lead.** When you let your toddler lead, you're letting her know her ideas are important.
- **Let the everyday be play.** Toddlers like to pretend they're doing everyday activities. Take turns and pretend with her. Your toddler is more likely to enjoy this kind of play if you let her know you are having fun.
- **Show and play.** Encourage pretend-play by using objects in different ways and watch creativity grow when a banana is used as a phone and a wooden spoon becomes a microphone.
- **Use active listening.** Listen when you are playing and give an occasional comment such as "Hmmm," or, "I see," or "And then what happened?" to broaden her imagination.

Creative play

Along with pretend-play, toddlers love to use their hands and minds to build and create. Toys like building blocks help eye/hand coordination and imaginary thinking, puzzles help build problem-solving skills, and creating art allows children to express themselves.

Brightly coloured blocks and puzzles with chunky pieces can help your toddler learn colours and are easiest for her little hands to use. With modelling clay or dough, paint and paper children can re-create things they experience in their world. You might not always be able to tell what it is, but the act of creating is more important than how it turns out.

What you can do: encouraging creative play

- **Play with puzzles.** Start with simple wooden puzzles with fewer than 10, large pieces. As your toddler's skill improves, you can introduce more complex puzzles.

- **It's about creating, not the creation.** Let your toddler figure out how to paint or build, but stay close and offer help if he gets frustrated. Get your child to tell you about what he has created, and encourage his efforts and imagination.

- **Great art is messy.** Create a special area where it is okay to make a mess. Protect furniture and clothing before your toddler gets started and look for the washable art supplies.

Toddler toys and activities

Toddlers usually play with a toy for only a few minutes before moving to the next one. Take a tip from quality childcare centres and only have some of your toys out at a time. Each week, rotate your toys to keep your child interested. Local toy-lending libraries can increase your choices without increasing your costs.

Toys and activities toddlers enjoy:
- Finger paints (pudding also works), crayons and paper
- Stringing games with spools or large beads
- Large interlocking blocks such as Duplo
- Dolls that can be dressed and doll beds and blankets
- Cars, boats, trains and planes
- Action figures
- Water play with plastic bottles or cups
- Simple puzzles and matching games

- Play dough and modeling clay
- Dustpan and brush, cups and bowls
- Sandbox and sandbox toys
- Ride-on toys
- Hats and caps for simple dressing up
- Singing songs while helping with chores, such as putting napkins on the table or putting toys away.

Feelings and emotions

The brain develops very rapidly in the toddler years, especially in the area responsible for emotions. Toddlers feel emotions intensely whether they're happy or sad, and it takes time for them to learn how to deal with these new feelings. It can be very confusing to them.

Emotional regulation

Toddlers need to learn to name their emotions. This is an important step in *emotional regulation* (learning how emotions make you feel and learning healthy ways of showing those emotions to others). When a child learns to regulate or control her emotions, she learns to:
- Recognize what she is feeling
- Show feelings in ways that don't hurt herself or others
- Cope with her emotions.

Learning to cope with emotions takes many years. By starting now, your toddler will be much more likely to get along well with other children and be more capable of coping with her emotions as an adult.

Give feelings a name

Toddlers need to know what feelings are before they can learn how to express or cope with them.

Help your toddler learn about feelings by:
- Giving them a name. For example, by saying, "I feel (angry, sad, frustrated or happy)."
- Encouraging him to use words rather than actions to express his feelings. For example saying, "I'm mad," instead of hitting.

Accept the feeling, limit the behaviour

As your toddler grows, build on his learning by *acknowledging* and *accepting* all his feelings—both the ones you are comfortable with (such as happiness) and the ones that might make you uncomfortable (such as anger)—even when you have to *limit your child's behaviour*.
- Acknowledge his feelings by saying "I see you are (angry, sad, frustrated, happy)."

- Accept his feelings by saying, "It is okay to be (angry, sad, frustrated, happy)."
- Limit behaviours by saying "It is not okay to (hit, bite, scream, throw things or pinch)."
- Give him options on what he can do instead, such as: telling you he's mad; walking away and calming down; taking a deep breath; or stamping his feet.

When you do these things, you help your child learn it is okay to have feelings and there are better ways to let people know about them.

Coping with emotions is one of the most important things your young child needs to learn. The benefits of helping your child learn about feeling are a lifetime of mental health and healthy relationships.

Over time and with your help, your child will learn to cope. Remember, you are a powerful role model—your child learns how to deal with his emotions by watching you. If you can calm yourself down and stay in control when you are angry, you can expect your child to learn that. If you are short-tempered and yell, your child will learn that is the way to express anger.

Many parents have trouble naming and dealing with their emotions, especially if they haven't learned how to do that as children or adults. *Growing Miracles* introduces you to many effective, positive ways to help you and your child deal with emotions and frustrations. You are your child's first and most important teacher. Help your child by getting the help you need if you have problems dealing with your emotions.

Temper tantrums

Temper tantrums are a normal and natural, although noisy and wrenching part of childhood. They can be distressing to children and parents alike. Some experts call temper tantrums *meltdowns*, and others call them *emotional sneezes*—a way for children to clear out conflicting feelings. Even calm and quiet children can have tantrums.

Temper tantrums are common during the toddler years and usually peak by the age of 3.

Anger and frustration are the biggest causes of tantrums, but illness, confusion, helplessness, hunger, loneliness, fear and too much excitement and activity can also lead to uncontrollable crying, yelling and thrashing about. Your child is more likely to have a tantrum when she is tired, hungry or rushed.

Children can learn that people do better when they feel better, and that calming down and cooling off can make them feel better. A child should not be punished for having a tantrum. She is simply learning how to deal with her emotions. She needs your help.

Children with too few limits or too many choices may become used to getting everything they want and can have a tantrum when suddenly faced with limits from other adults. Power struggles and tantrums are common when toddlers think they can do more than they can.

Occasional tantrums are normal, but if your child has frequent or long tantrums, talk to your doctor or public health nurse.

Tantrums do have a purpose. By expressing their feelings, children learn to deal with their feelings. With guidance and reassurance, you can help your child understand and learn how to show her feelings in healthier ways.

Preventing tantrums

Not every tantrum can be avoided, but many can be prevented if you:

- Know what's normal for your child's age and better understand what he can and cannot do.
- Learn what frustrates him.
- Relieve your child's stress with physical activity.
- Respect his eating and sleeping routines. Don't try to do too many things in to one day.
- Watch for early warning signs. You can often see a child's frustration building before an actual tantrum begins. That's the best time to distract, change activity, or take a break.
- Help him learn his feelings have names and that there are better ways to show them.
- Find your balance. Know when to set limits, offer choices, be flexible and be firm.
- Give attention to your toddler's positive behaviour. This is most effective when you react right away. For example, as soon as you hang up the phone say, "Thank you for playing quietly while I was talking."

Coping with tantrums

Tantrums have many causes, so you need a few strategies to deal with the different types. Whatever the cause, when your toddler has a tantrum, stay calm. If you lose your temper, yell, scream or react physically, your child learns to react the same way.

What you can do: toddler tantrums

- If your child's tantrum is due to frustration, tiredness, or feeling overwhelmed, follow the suggestions in *Taming a tantrum* on page 111.

- As your toddler gets older, she may have a tantrum because she wants something she can't have. In this case, you can try ignoring the tantrum (but not your child). Make sure your child is safe and that she cannot hurt anyone, stay close by, but busy yourself with something else. Pay attention again once you hear the tantrum winding down.

- If you are in a public place (a grocery store, a movie theatre or a playgroup), take her to a quiet place and stay with her until she calms down.

- Remain kind and firm and don't give in. Reassure your child that you understand her feelings. Let her know you will stop her from hurting herself or others.

- Once she has calmed down, help her describe her feelings (mad, sad, happy or scared). Suggest one or two other ways she can deal with her feelings. This helps her understand that her feelings are acceptable, but her behaviour has limits. Some children like to be held during a temper tantrum. Others prefer a hug after they've calmed down. Give your child a way to come back with dignity.

- Time outs (see page 166) are not advised for children less than 3 years of age.

- Remind yourself that this is a stage and it too will pass, and that the coping skills you teach her now will be for life.

Physical punishment

Some parents think spanking is a way to teach their children how to behave. Some parents pull their children's hair or pinch their ears for the same reasons. All of these things are called *physical punishment*. While physical punishment may seem to stop annoying behaviour for the moment, it does nothing to teach children what to do in the future. It also has harmful long-term effects on children.

Parents who spank or hit find that as their children grow older, a smack on the bottom or tweak on the ear is no longer enough and they begin to hit their children harder. When this happens, children can be seriously injured.

Spanking, hitting and other types of physical punishment leave children fearful, angry and powerless. Studies show children who are physically punished tend to have more behaviour problems (such as anxiety and aggression) than those who aren't. These children are also more likely to hit others, as they believe that hitting solves problems.

Effective discipline is about teaching, not about punishing. You do not need to use physical punishment. Even if you were physically punished when growing up, *Growing Miracles* can help you find more positive ways to help your child learn how to behave.

Your toddler's world

Your toddler's world is growing by leaps and bounds. Toddlers are very active, always walking, running, jumping and climbing. As they move away from their parents, they move towards other children and start interacting with them. The constant movement of toddlers means they need active supervision whenever they are awake. Eyes on and hands near are good practices to follow when parenting toddlers.

Getting along with others

Most times, toddlers like to get along with others. Your toddler is probably eager to do what you do. He may copy or help with simple household chores, especially if you have child-size versions of everyday things such as brooms, dishes and shovels. He also begins to play on his own for short periods, but still needs to have you close by. Around the age of 2, he likes to be with other children.

Playing with others

Young toddlers play by themselves, with their parents and other familiar adults. When they are with other children, toddlers like to watch and often copy what they see. Toddlers play beside one another, but usually not together as they are not able to share. This is a normal stage called *parallel play*.

As your toddler grows and learns, she starts to play with other children. This is called *cooperative play*, and usually happens after age 3.

In cooperative play, children learn to work and solve problems together, and develop their social skills. They learn to share, take turns and be part of a team or group. This type of play becomes more organized as children become preschoolers and new schoolers.

Toddler Property Laws

If I like it, it's mine.
If it's in my hand, it's mine.
If I can take it away from you, it's mine.
If I had it a little while ago, it's mine.
If it's mine, it must never appear to be yours in any way.
If we are building something together, all of the pieces are mine.
If it looks just like mine, it's mine.
If I think it's mine, it's mine.
If I give it to you, and change my mind later, it's mine.
If it's broken, it's yours!
—Unknown

Sharing

Toddlers are just figuring out who they are. They define themselves by what belongs to them (such as my arm, my eyes, my books and my teddy). At times you may feel your toddler thinks everything belongs to her! Your toddler needs to learn ownership first. Once she is comfortable with who she is and what belongs to her, she can then learn to share.

What you can do: learning to share

- Give your toddler the chance to be with other children
- Sit nearby on the floor when toddlers are playing together so you can step in quickly if needed.
- Teach and model sharing, but don't expect it.
- Put special toys away when friends come to visit.

Learning social skills

Social skills don't develop naturally; they need to be learned. Because each child is unique, some may struggle more than others to learn positive behaviour and how to get along with others.

No is normal

Saying "NO!" doesn't mean your toddler is defiant. It may just be his way of telling you he wants to do things by himself. For example, if you say, "Let's get your coat on," and he blurts out, "NO!" it could be he wants to do it on his own.

Sometimes when you say "NO!" less, your child will too. If your child asks to go outside to play, you can say "Sure, as soon as we are done lunch." Or if your toddler wants to touch a special ornament, you could say (as you put it out of reach and give him a non-breakable one), "That one can break, but you can play with this one."

Children learn what they live

You help your child learn to cooperate when you are positive, cooperative, polite and pay attention.

Toddlers may have challenging moments, but for the most part, they like to please you. All children need their parents' attention. If they only get it when they do something wrong, children learn to misbehave to get the attention they need. If attention is given when they behave in ways parents like, children learn positive ways to connect. Encouragement and positive attention (with smiles, hugs, please, thank you and comments on what they are doing) help your child learn how to behave.

Help your child learn positive behaviour by:
• Teaching him about respect and treating him with respect
• Solving problems with nonviolent solutions
• Setting a good example.

Let them do what they can

Toddlers learn by doing. They want to try everything, but not everything is safe. Know what your little one can do and encourage him to try what he can. When you stay close by, you can quickly help if needed.

Giving toddlers choices helps them feel like they have a bit of control in their life. Limit the choice to two things, as long as you can accept both options. For example, you can give the choice of wearing a red hat or a blue hat (as long as both are available), or reading a book or singing a song before bed. Not all things have a choice, such as staying in his car seat, brushing his teeth or going to childcare. When no choice exists, don't give one. Rather than asking "Do you want to go to bed now?" simply say, "It's time for bed."

Setting limits

Dealing with a child's behaviour is one of a parent's toughest jobs. Young children seldom misbehave to annoy their parents. Many reasons can lead toddlers to act the way they do. What parents think is misbehaviour might just be normal toddler behaviour, such as:

- Actively exploring everything around them. For example, when they want to know what's in the cereal box, they happily dump the contents on the floor.
- Figuring out what they can and can't do by testing limits.
- Still learning the difference between acceptable and unacceptable behaviour.
- Thinking it is a game (when you say no, and they wait until you are watching and do it again).
- Being tired, lonely, bored, over-excited, ill, frustrated, hungry or thirsty.

As a parent, you teach your child by setting limits on what he can and cannot do, and this includes his behaviour. Use simple language your child can understand and follow these steps:

- Tell your child what your limits are and why they are important. Be very clear about what you expect.
- When your child stays inside your limits, tell him you are pleased and give him positive encouragement.
- When your child goes over the limit you have set, tell him what he did and why he can't do it, and what you want him to do instead (for example, "No pulling the cat's tail. It hurts her. Pat her nicely, like this.")

Be kind and firm. Your child needs to understand why he must not behave in a certain way and what he can do instead. Consider your child's age and abilities to see if your expectations are realistic.

Solving problems

Toddlers are too young to learn all the skills of problem solving, but you can help show her problems can be solved. If she spills her mashed peas on the floor, you can say, "Oh-oh, we have a problem. What do we need to do? We have to clean it up with a cloth," as you clean it up.

When your child helps you solve the problem, she begins to learn that when she's made a mistake or has a problem, she can solve it (also see *Dealing with problems* on page 175 and *Problem solving* on page 176.)

Making it easier to behave

You can avoid many problems with your children if you make it easier for them to behave in ways you want. How you communicate and how you set up your home can prevent many problems before they start and create a more peaceful setting.

Communicating

Toddlers are more likely to be cooperative when they are approached positively. Try to limit how many times you say no—try to find other ways to get around it.

Tone of voice, body language, listening, eye contact, paying attention, giving attention and the way we talk to our children are all parts of how we communicate. Communication can either build or breakdown a relationship. Some communication skills that can help you build your relationship with your toddler, include:

- **Keep it simple.** Young children need simple rules and limits suited to their age. Keep information short and simple in words your child can understand.
- **Get down to her level.** If you want to get your child's attention, get down to his level. Squat down so your eyes are level and tell him what he needs to know. For example, if he has run out into the street, tell him, "Cars cannot see you and you can get run over." Don't assume he knows these things.
- **Match tone to concern.** If you are concerned, sound concerned. If you want your child to stop throwing his carrots, say it firmly, but without yelling.
- **Show pleasure.** Share your pleasure and happiness with your toddlers when he acts in acceptable ways or learns new things. When you are happy, match your voice to your mood.

- **Actively listen.** When your child talks to you, turn and face him. Listen to what he is saying and the thoughts and feelings that he is trying to express.
- **Time to change.** Toddlers like and thrive on routine. Let them know if there is something coming up that is different. Toddlers find it hard to stop doing things they enjoy. Give them time to change to a different activity

Make your child at home

Your child's surroundings affect his behaviour. To make your child feel safe and welcome, make your home:

- **Child proof . . .** remove and/or lock up anything that could harm your child.
- **. . . and child friendly.** Make his surroundings interesting and accessible. Use a solid stepstool to help him reach the sink. Have coat hooks where he can reach them. Create a special place for books and toys. Put his things at his level. He is more likely to put his books away if he can reach the shelf.

What you can do: encouraging cooperation

- **Have reasonable expectations.** Know what toddlers can and cannot do.
- **Have fun.** Toddlers like to please and be with you.
- **Be positive.** Positive requests are more effective than negative commands. For example, your child is more likely to respond to, "Please use your spoon," than "Don't eat with your fingers."
- **Give limited choices**—between two things (both options you can live with) whenever you can.
- **Keep it interesting.** Rotate toys and books every week or so. You don't need to spend a lot of money on toys and books. Check out your local public library or toy lending library.
- **Prepare for what's coming.** Give your child a five-minute warning when you want her to change activities. "In five minutes, we have to go. It's time to start cleaning up."
- **Build the routine.** Make cleanup fun with a special song. If you do it every time playtime is over, your child comes to expect cleanup is part of play.

- **Distract.** If you don't like what your child is doing, give her something else to do. This is an easy and effective way to deal with your toddler. It avoids conflict and constantly having to say, "No!" or "Don't do that!"

- **Redirect.** Sometimes what your child is doing isn't wrong, but she's doing it in the wrong place or with the wrong things. Maybe she's decided to paint the bathroom floor or give your plants a glass of milk. You can change the place or the things and explain why.

Change the setting

Before things get out of control, end them. When a play date is not going well, or you are in a store and your toddler is not cooperating, leave. Sometimes just changing your child's surroundings changes her behaviour. You may need to leave the grocery store before you have everything on your list and take him to a playground to burn off some energy.

Leaving may frustrate you if you are not ready to leave, but the lesson is too important to ignore. Tell your child you are not able to stay when he chooses not to cooperate (for example he needs to play without hitting or stay with you in the store).

Resist the urge to punish. Be kind and firm. Let him know he can try again another day. Have patience. Your child learns with experience and as he grows older.

A new baby in the house

For many toddlers, learning to get along with others includes learning to get along with a new brother or sister. If your family is expecting a new addition, your toddler will be more enthusiastic about the baby's arrival if you prepare him in advance.

Before your baby is born, tell your toddler what to expect: that new babies need a lot of special care and attention. Use a doll to show him what caring for a baby looks like. Let him know that babies can't do things (like run and play and climb and read books) like toddlers can.

It can be a big adjustment for toddlers when a new baby suddenly takes attention away from them. Toddlers need your attention (as do all children), and when they see that a baby gets a lot of attention, they may start to act like a baby too. Let your child continue to act this way without drawing attention to it. At the same time, look for ways to give him positive support for being a toddler.

You can let your toddler know he is secure and loved—and make him feel loved and good about himself—by spending some time alone with him each day. Look for little ways that he can help (getting you a diaper, singing a song to the baby). This approach quickly helps toddlers realize being an older brother or sister is special too.

Make sure your toddler can't hurt your new baby, even accidentally. Toddlers often express their feelings physically and don't realize that their actions can be harmful. Never leave a toddler alone with a baby.

Be patient. Just as it takes you time to get used to your new baby, it takes time for siblings to adjust to one another.

Protecting your toddler

Toddlers are active, curious and very mobile. Because they can now climb, slide, swing, open doors and move very quickly, they are much more likely to get into dangerous situations. As they are impulsive by nature, you cannot rely on them to always remember or follow safety rules; they need active supervision. Active supervision means being within an arm's reach at all time, paying close attention and anticipating hazards when your child is playing or exploring.

Playgrounds are designed for children of all ages. Find one with equipment that is right for your toddler's age and size. This includes easy climbers, low stairs and platforms, small slides and tunnels, activity panels and playhouses. If your child cannot reach equipment, it is too advanced for her.

Toddlers and preschoolers are still developing their strength, balance, coordination and climbing skills. They sometimes try things they aren't quite ready to do, especially when playing around older children and with adults. They may soon be ready for a tricycle. By law in Alberta, anyone under the age of 18 (toddlers and babies included) must wear a helmet in a bike trailer or on a bicycle or tricycle. When you wear a helmet too, your toddler is more likely to adopt this habit for life.

Falls are the leading cause of hospital visits for childhood injuries. The most serious falls for children aged 1 to 4 years are down stairs, from windows, balconies or other high spots.

Scalds and burns can happen in an instant. If you haven't already done so, lower the temperature of your hot water heater to warm (49 °C or 120 °F). Keep your toddler safely out of the way when you are using the stove or oven. Be careful with microwaves as they often heat and cook food unevenly, leaving hot spots in throughout the food. Stir food thoroughly before serving.

Choking and poisoning are real hazards to children under the age of 5 because they explore by putting things in their mouths. They do not understand that this can be dangerous. Toys should be suited to your child's age and have no small parts. Latex balloons are not toys—a piece of broken balloon can choke a child. Have fun and stay healthy while playing outside.

See *The great outdoors* on page 30 on how to protect your child from the sun and bugs.

Make vehicle travel safe for your child. Always use an approved car seat designed for your child's age and size. Children 12 and under safest in the back seat.

What you can do: create a safer environment

- **Prevent falls.** Use protective devices such as stair gates and safety straps. Always use the safety strap in high chairs, strollers and grocery carts; insist your child sit down. Put outdoor play equipment on a soft surface (such as sand, pea gravel, rubber mats or wood chips) for soft landings and stay close to your playing toddler. Toddlers are too young to be playing unattended inside or out. Use safety latches (that can be released by an adult) on windows that can open.

- **Prevent scalds and burns.** Lower your water temperature. Use lids on hot drinks (like coffee and tea) even at home. Keep them away from your child. Cook food on the back burners of your stove with the handles of pots and pans turned in. Always test the temperature of your child's food before you serve it to make sure it is not too hot. Use placemats instead of tablecloths to prevent your toddler from grabbing the tablecloth and pulling hot liquids or food onto herself. Place a safety gate around your gas or electric fireplace, even if it is enclosed.

- **Play safe.** Choose age-appropriate, safe toys. Do not let your toddler play with latex balloons. Have your child wear a helmet when on a bike (or in a bike trailer) and take it off to play (for example, on playground equipment). Follow age guidelines for using sunscreen and insect repellent. Teach your children to play in the shade.

- **Remove dangerous items.** Lock cleaning solutions, matches, cosmetics and medications in cupboards out of your child's reach. Remove poisonous plants from your home and yard. Call the Alberta Poison Centre at 403-944-1414 if you think your child has been poisoned.

- **Travel smart.** Match your child's car seat to his size and age:
  - Use a rear-facing seat until your child is at least 1 year old **and** weighs 9 kg (20 lbs.). Then use a forward-facing car seat appropriate for your child's height and weight until your child is at least 18 kg (40 lbs.).
  - Once your child weighs 18 kg (40 lbs.), use a booster seat so the car's seat belt fits properly. Booster seats are recommended until children are 9 years old or weigh 36 kg (80 lbs.).
  - Know how to install and use your baby's car seat.

    First, consult the instructions that come with your child's safety seat and the instructions in your vehicle owner's manual.

    Next, take the appropriate Child Safety Seat Yes Test (available from your community health centre or at www.albertahealthservices.ca).

    Call Health Link Alberta for information on car seat classes offered in your community or if you have other questions.

For more information on keeping your child safe and healthy at any age, see *Protecting your child* on page 26 and *Keeping your child healthy* on page 32.

Teach safety rules

Just like any other rules, safety rules need to be taught. You will need to repeat them over and over for many years, but this is how your toddler learns. Teach and model the rules, but do not rely on your toddler to follow them consistently.

Look for chances to teach safety throughout your day. Teach your toddler to hold your hand and stay close to you when walking along roads or in parking lots. Teach him never to play in driveways, garages or streets. The safety rules he learns now help him make safer choices when he is older.

Caring for you

Toddlers are curious, delightful, exciting and always trying new things. In short, toddlers are busy! As a parent, you may find the toddler years exhausting. When you deal with your own emotions and needs, you are more likely to have the energy and patience you will need to be the parent you want to be.

Power struggles

A *power struggle* is an argument, or battle-of-wills, that can happen when you want your child to do something and he wants to do something else. When two people want different things and both want to get their way, power struggles happen.

Understanding normal development can help you understand your child's behaviour. A toddler's behaviour is most often driven by the need to have some control in his life, the need to do everything by himself.

As a parent, you have more power than your child because you are older, bigger and have more thinking skills. Also, you control the environment your child lives in. It is your responsibility as a parent to use this power with wisdom, respect and consideration to help your child learn, rather than to force him to obey.

The three things you cannot make a child do—sleep, eat and go to the toilet (pee or poop)—are most often the areas of power struggles for parents of toddlers. Power struggles can be very frustrating, but can often be avoided. The ideas in this book help you with these challenging situations: see *Sleeping* on page 125, *The feeding relationship* on page 123 and *Toddlers and toilets* on page 128.

Keeping your cool

Stress often simmers, but anger can explode.

It can be tough to keep your cool around a toddler who's just put a roll of toilet paper in the toilet or is painting a picture with mashed potatoes on the dining room table. To defuse a burst of anger, you can:

- **Breathe.** Take a deep breath and slowly count to 10. Don't think about the problem, just concentrate on breathing, counting and calming down.
- **Walk away.** As long as your child and anyone near him are safe, simply leave the room and gather your thoughts.
- **Be positive.** Your child is seldom trying to annoy you. He's just growing, experimenting and discovering.
- **Understand.** Toddlers don't know their limits yet. They're still learning what they can and can't do. In their minds, your new lipstick is just another crayon.
- **Ask for help.** All parents need a little help sometimes. Before you reach the breaking point, ask a friend, relative or caregiver to give you a break.
- **Learn to cope with stress.** Parents of toddlers are more prone to stress because their child is always on the go, and needs to be closely monitored all the time. See *Balancing life as a parent* on page 11 for ways to control stress so it doesn't control you.

Build your skills

It's easier to deal with toddlers if you have a variety of parenting tools for different situations. Shaping a life is like building a house and begins with a solid foundation (like knowledge) and the right tools (like the parenting strategies in this book). Parenting programs are a great way to meet new friends and build your parenting skills. Parenting programs are for everyone. For more information, call Health Link Alberta or 211.

Preschoolers
3 TO 5 YEARS

*There are few successful adults who were
not first successful children.*

— Alexander Chase

Growing with your preschooler

As they enter their preschool years, children quickly develop their own identities. As they do, they know what they like and what they dislike. Preschoolers' emotions tend to be more stable and predictable than toddlers' emotions. As preschoolers understand their emotions better, they start telling you their feelings and opinions.

Socially, preschoolers want to play with other children and, over time, they learn how to share and play cooperatively. Physically, preschool children become more able and coordinated in their movements. They use most of their energy becoming better at everything they do.

The preschool years are an intense period of speech and language development. At 3 years old, children speak three- to five-word sentences. By the time they are 5, they are telling complex and lengthy stories. Preschoolers love to imitate, sing, recite rhymes and have fun with words. They have vivid imaginations and sometimes have difficulty telling what is real and what is fantasy.

Preschoolers play, work and live life to the fullest. One of the main things preschoolers learn is *initiative*, the ability to make their own plans, or act on their own without waiting to be told what to do. They feel a real sense of accomplishment and satisfaction in activities, but they may lack confidence in their abilities. When given the chance to develop their skills, preschoolers learn to feel capable. This is an essential building block for healthy self-esteem. When your preschooler makes a blanket tent under the coffee table, builds a cardboard fort in the backyard, or puts her books away without you asking, you'll know she's developing initiative.

These types of learning and play activities help prepare children for school and classroom learning. If preschool is an option, choose one that focuses on creativity and social skills. The most important things to foster at this age are excitement about learning and the ability to get along with others.

Your preschooler's body

Between 3 and 5 years of age, preschoolers gain about 1 to 2 kg (2 to 4 lbs.) a year and grow about 2.5 to 5 cm (1 to 2 in.) a year. Their legs and arms tend to grow more than their body.

Preschoolers' control of both their small and large muscles continues to develop at a rapid pace. Preschoolers move with more purpose and confidence than toddlers—partly because they repeat movements, skills and activities until they can do them really well and partly because they have more strength and better balance.

This means preschoolers can run, jump and climb (forward and backwards) as well as swing, skip and hop on one foot much better than when they were wobbly toddlers. Preschoolers can also walk down stairs, one foot at a time, without help, although they need to learn to hold onto a railing for safety.

The more active children are the better able they become at moving with skill, efficiency and confidence. Stay close by to see their pride at being able to do something all by themselves.

At mealtimes, preschoolers are tidier when feeding themselves and can use a spoon and fork. Some children this age are also able to use a knife, but need to learn to use it safely.

Drawing, scribbling and creating crafts help preschoolers get better at using their fine motor skills. You can expect your preschooler to copy and draw shapes such as circles, squares and triangles. He will also draw his first people (with simple lines and shapes for the head, body, legs and arms), print his first letters and use children's scissors. He can pick up small objects and put them into small openings in one smooth movement. By watching your preschooler carefully at this age, you can often tell if he's right- or left-handed.

Eager to be independent, young preschoolers can usually dress and undress themselves. Doing up and undoing buttons are complex skills for young preschoolers and something they may not be able to do well until at least age 4. Your preschooler may also want to do more of his personal hygiene (such as brushing his teeth, combing his hair, and washing his hands, face and body), but you'll need to help to make sure these jobs are done thoroughly.

As preschoolers get older, their eyes, ears and hands work together with increasing skill. They can clap along to a song's rhythm, and throw and catch a small ball more accurately.

At 4 to 5 years of age, preschoolers show lots of expression, by rolling and moving their eyes, when they talk. Some can even wink or close one eye.

Preschoolers become very interested in what it means to be a boy or a girl. As your child develops an increased awareness of his sexuality, you may notice he is fascinated with his body and the physical differences between boys and girls. Preschoolers often explore their bodies by *playing house* or *playing doctor* with a playmate.

Children touch their own genitals just as they touch other parts of their bodies. They may find that this touch feels good. This is normal exploration for children and how they learn about how the whole body works. These are ideal times to talk about correct names for body parts and socially acceptable ways of touching.

You are your child's main source of information about sexuality. Innocent questions (such as, "Where do babies come from?" "Why don't I have a penis?" or "How do girls go pee?") need simple, honest answers. Keep it brief—when children want more information, they will usually ask. Being open and frank now with your child helps you both deal with sexuality and sexual health with more ease later. For more information on talking about sexuality with your child, see the Alberta Health Services website or call Health Link Alberta.

Eating

Preschool children are busy all day long. They need food at regular times. Large meals are difficult for them as their appetites are smaller than adults and they find it hard to sit for very long. Having three meals and three snacks spaced evenly throughout the day, whether at home or away, suits their needs much better.

Preschoolers love their own ideas and plans, and this can be seen in everything they do. When it comes to eating, preschoolers like to choose what they eat, and may want to help prepare and serve food. It's common for them to want only certain foods, or to love something one day and hate it the next. You may worry that your child is being a fussy or picky eater, but she may just be testing her limits and making her own choices.

Remember, the feeding relationship sets healthy eating habits for life. Preschoolers are still responsible for choosing to eat and how much they eat. Parents are still responsible for what, when and where food is offered. For more information on each of your roles, see *The feeding relationship* on page 122.

If your preschooler is always saying, "I'm not hungry," don't force food on her. As long as she's not filling up on empty calories (foods like chips and pop that leave no room for the healthy food she needs to grow), she will eat when she is hungry. Continue to offer well-balanced meals and regularly planned snacks from the four food groups in Canada's Food Guide. If you are concerned about your preschooler's eating, talk to your doctor or public health nurse.

Family meals are always important times for families to connect. Eating together promotes a healthy feeding relationship with everyone in the family and gives families time together to talk about their day. These daily times together prevent relationship problems now and in the future.

Rewarding with food

Food is nourishment and necessary for life. It should not be used to reward or punish behaviour. Children should not feel that they have to earn food, or that it could be taken away as punishment. When children are rewarded with food, they can confuse eating with encouragement and love. Punishment can cause children to lose their trust in the world. When food and behaviour are linked, children learn an unhealthy relationship with eating that creates a lifetime of problems. For alternatives to using rewards, bribes and punishments, see *Your toddler's world* on page 142 and *Your preschooler's world* on page 171.

Modern manners

While many manners from centuries past have been relaxed or abandoned, a few simple table manners can make meals more enjoyable. Decide which manners you feel are important for your family to follow. When you use them consistently, your preschooler will learn to use them too.

Eating away from home

Not so long ago, eating out was a special treat. For some people it still is, but for a growing number of people in today's busy world, eating out is a matter of convenience not celebration.

Although eating out (or ordering in) is convenient, fast food, takeout food and restaurant food can be much higher in fat, salt, sugar and calories than food made and cooked at home.

As well, for young children, eating out creates several challenges. They find it hard to sit at a table for longer than 15 or 20 minutes. They may be distracted in restaurants and eat either too much or too little. They may also become used to *super-size* meals or foods high in fat and salt.

Some ways you can make dining out more nutritious include:
- Choose restaurants with healthy choices such as lean or grilled meats, poultry or fish, steamed or sautéed vegetables and fruit for dessert.

- Avoid super-size portions and second helpings.
- Choose tomato-based sauces rather than cream-based sauces for pasta.
- Limit fried and deep-fried foods.
- Ask for dressings and sauces on the side.
- Encourage your child to try more than just hamburgers, fries and chicken fingers. Consider ordering from the regular menu, not just the children's menu. You and your child can share an adult-sized meal. You can also ask for a half-serving or take leftover food home.
- Limit pop and slushy drinks, which are very high in sugar. Better choices include milk, chocolate milk, chocolate milk mixed with white milk, vegetable and fruit juices or sparkling water with a twist of lemon or lime or a splash of fruit juice. Make drinks *special* with a slice of fruit, a decorative umbrella or a straw.

Under the right conditions, eating out can help preschoolers learn how people behave in social settings. The right conditions are when your child is rested and in a good mood, not when your child is tired, cranky, restless or frustrated.

Sometimes, your child's mood and energy level can change in the middle of a meal. When your child is first learning these new social skills, you need to be prepared to leave quickly. Trying to get your child to behave or wait in a restaurant when he's overwhelmed can make matters worse. Be kind and firm. Let him know it is time to go. Your child learns you mean what you say when you follow through. This can be inconvenient and annoying, but you usually only need to do it once.

Resist the urge to punish. Let your child know that there will be other meals out and that you will try again another day. When your child knows what to expect and what's expected of him, eating out becomes more relaxed and pleasant for everyone.

What you can do: making eating out enjoyable

- Pretend-play or practice at home first. This helps your child learn what's expected of him and what he can expect. Think of things to do while you're waiting for food (colouring or playing *I Spy* or cards).
- Stay in if your child is tired or ready for a nap or bed.
- Bring some goodies. A small box of crayons and a notebook, a few slices of apple, a bag of carrot sticks or a book can all keep your child busy and satisfied until the food arrives.

- Have reasonable expectations. Choose child-friendly restaurants with high chairs, booster seats and a tolerance for children's needs and moods. This doesn't mean just eating at places where food comes in Styrofoam containers and paper wrappers, but you might have to give up candlelight and crisp linen for a while.

Teeth and oral health

Preschoolers usually have all 20 of their baby teeth. Their baby teeth usually begin to fall out and their permanent teeth begin to grow when they are 5 or older.

By now, your preschooler may feel he's big enough to brush his own teeth, but you still need to supervise his brushing and flossing until he's 8 years old. (See *How to brush* on page 124 and *Using dental floss* on page 99).

Preschoolers often suck their thumb or fingers or a soother for comfort, but if your child sucks his thumb excessively, it can affect his mouth and teeth. Encourage your child to give up the habit before his permanent teeth come in. By encouraging your child, rather than punishing, you prevent damage to his self-esteem.

What you can do: kicking the (thumb) habit

- Offer a substitute for thumb, fingers or soother, such as a soft blanket or a favourite toy.
- Limit comfort sucking to certain times or places, such as bedtime or in your child's room.

- Encourage by redirecting behaviour and gently remind at other times. For example, if your child sucks when watching TV, she may be doing it out of habit, not for comfort. Try not to pay too much attention to it, however, as this can have the opposite effect of increasing the behaviour.
- Be patient. Like any habit, it takes time to change.

Sleeping

On average, young children sleep a little less with each passing year until, as teens, they need eight to 10 hours a night. At 3 years old, children sleep about 12 hours a day and by 5 years old, they need about 11 hours. Many children nap for about an hour a day until they're 5 or older. When children get the sleep they need, they are happier and healthier.

Your preschooler is probably not getting enough sleep if:
- He regularly falls asleep in the car or while watching television at any time of the day.
- You have to wake him every morning.
- He seems cranky during the day.
- He naps more than once a day.

For more information on sleep routines and keeping young children in bed, see *What you can do: peaceful bedtimes* on page 128.

Toilet teaching

At 3 years old, your preschooler may be just learning how to use the toilet or may be very comfortable with using it. For information and tips on toilet teaching, see *Toddlers and toilets* on page 128.

Setbacks and bedwetting

- You can expect bedwetting, occasional accidents or lapses when your child is learning to use the toilet.
- Girls tend to be ready for toilet teaching before boys. Some boys may not be ready until they are 3-1/2 years old.
- Bedwetting is common in preschoolers and it is not something they do on purpose. Use a waterproof cover to protect your child's mattress. Most children outgrow bedwetting by 5 or 6. Talk to your doctor or public health nurse if you are concerned.

Your preschooler's mind

As preschoolers discover their creativity and develop their resourcefulness, they get very excited about the world they live in. With their sense of wonder awakened, preschoolers want to do everything for themselves and constantly want to know, "Why?"

The preschool years are an important and energetic time of learning. This is when your child develops the ability to act on her own behalf and a sense of "I can do it!" Your child now knows she is a separate and independent person. She wants to experience and do things for herself. Like all preschoolers, she learns best by doing.

Learning experiences are everywhere because preschoolers are interested in everything. There are times preschoolers seem happy watching the same cartoon show dozens of times or drawing the same stick person over and over again, but they need a variety of new experiences for their learning to grow.

At this stage, your preschooler also needs activities that are indoors, outdoors and increasingly with other children. Too many new experiences, however, can be overwhelming. The key is balance. Your child also needs quiet time to learn how to entertain herself and play on her own. A little boredom can be a great motivator for creative play.

Vision

Of all our senses, vision plays the biggest role in learning at this age. The pathways for vision are still forming in a young child's brain. Vision should not be taken for granted.

Because your preschooler thinks everyone sees the same way he does, he has no way of knowing if his eyesight is bad—but you do. If your child has any of the following signs, have an optometrist check his vision:

- Often rubs eyes or blinks
- Covers one eye
- Has a short attention span
- Often daydreams
- Has poor eye/hand coordination
- Avoids close work such as reading or crafts
- Sits very close to the TV
- Has many headaches
- Tilts head.

Not all vision problems have symptoms or warnings. Regular visits to the optometrist are the best way to protect your child's vision.

Learning speech and language

Expect to see almost staggering growth in your preschooler's language skills and abilities as your child learns that words represent things in his world.

At 3 years old, your preschooler:
- Has a word for almost everything
- Is understood by others about 75 to 100 per cent of the time
- Knows the colours red, blue and yellow
- May talk more often and longer
- Likes to use nonsense (and sometimes naughty) words, rhymes and songs with actions
- Asks questions to get information, "Why?" "Where's the puppy?" or "What is that?"

At 4 years old, your preschooler:
- Observes and recognizes her surroundings
- Talks about places, objects or people she's seen
- Likes to look at new things and places
- Uses sentences with five or more words
- Is understood most of the time
- Can tell stories and talk about what she's done
- Listens and follows three-step directions, such as, "Get your shoes, put them on and meet me by the door."
- Asks lots of questions
- Can probably count to 10
- Draws circles and squares, and people with up to four body parts.
- Knows her age and may know her full name and address
- May start using slang words such as *cool* or *gross*
- Understands opposites, such as *same* and *different, hot* and *cold, in* and *out*
- Understands *under, beside, in front* and *behind.*

As their brain development continues, preschoolers start to learn some *abstract concepts* (thoughts and ideas about things they can't directly see, hear, taste, smell or touch). Examples of abstract concepts are time, relationships and feelings. As preschoolers learn this way of thinking, they also become able to wait and share. They learn that it feels good to be nice to people and that others may have completely different feelings from theirs.

Preschoolers are great storytellers. They like to talk (a lot!) and love to tell jokes even if their humour doesn't always make sense. Preschoolers don't always know the difference between reality and fantasy.

Academic learning really takes hold in the preschooler years. Your preschooler increasingly connects language with thinking. At this age, she can learn to be creative, to observe cause and effect, and to begin solving problems. You help her do these things when you read and play with her, show her you understand, and kindly and firmly set limits. When your child starts childcare, a playgroup, preschool or nursery school, her circle of friends grows, but your influence and guidance remain as important as ever.

The foundations of literacy

Talking and listening are the foundations for the literacy skills of reading and writing—skills that your child will need to be successful at school.

To promote reading and writing, you can:

- Encourage your preschooler to share what he's learned and experienced. Let him find his own words and complete his own thoughts. He needs to experiment and become familiar with sharing his thoughts, using new words and practising grammar.

- Ask your child questions and wait for his answers. *Open-ended* questions allow your child to answer with a sentence or a story rather than a one-word answer such as yes or no. In everyday conversations, you can use simple questions such as, "What happened?" "What did you think about that?" or "What did you do?" Asking more specific questions also encourages your child to think and talk. For example, ask, "What happened when the bear ran into the river?" rather than "Did the bear get wet when he ran into the river?"

- Make family meals a time to sit down together so your children learn to follow conversations, and take turns talking and listening.

- Read every day and read often. Most children love a bedtime story, but reading time can be any time of the day. Preschoolers love books and stories with pictures, rhymes and repetition, such as Dr. Seuss.

- Run your finger along the words so your child begins to connect the sound and look of words. This also shows children the direction of reading. Whether it is from left to right, right to left or from top to bottom, help your child begin to learn the form of your written language.

- Let your child see that you're interested in reading by getting and reading your own books as well. Children who see others around them reading often copy them.

What you can do: promoting reading and writing

- Visit libraries or bookstores regularly.

- Create a spot for books—in your living room, bedrooms, bathrooms and vehicles—anywhere you or your child can take a few minutes to read.

- Connect to stories by talking about your child's own experiences. For example, if you are reading a story about the zoo, you can ask, "Remember when we saw a giraffe at the zoo?"

- Talk with your child about the print you see. Print is everywhere (on cereal boxes, traffic signs, logos, store and restaurant signs, advertising, flyers and even toys). Point it out to him.
- Have paper, crayons, markers and paints on hand. Make time during the day to draw pictures, make signs, develop lists and write cards together. When your child helps, he learns one of the many ways language can be used. Early scribbling is important for later writing.
- Write words on the sidewalk in chalk or in the sand or snow with a stick.

Feelings and emotions

Understanding and expressing emotions

Young preschoolers understand and use words for emotions such as *happy*, *sad*, *mad*, *scared* and *excited*. As they get older, they begin to learn and feel more complex emotions such as *jealous*, *pride* and *guilt*.

Help your child build his understanding of feelings. Continue to give new emotions a name—it helps your child connect to what he feels. Let him know it is okay to have feelings (it helps him feel understood) as you help him learn to express his feelings properly.

Preschoolers are able to control their emotions more than toddlers because they have started to learn how to deal with frustration. Preschoolers are less physical and impulsive than toddlers. They can now learn to think and observe before acting and to wait for short periods. As they learn about their own feelings, they begin to understand that other people may have feelings that are different from their own.

Preschoolers can also begin to use language to talk themselves through difficult situations. Children develop these skills through their early relationships with the important people in their lives.

Even so, emotions can easily overwhelm preschoolers. At times, preschoolers still have tantrums, and show their anger and frustration the same way they did when they were younger: physically and loudly. By age 4, this should be the exception, not the norm. If you are concerned about your child's emotional development, talk to your doctor or public health nurse.

Time out

Time out can be an effective parenting tool when it is used to help children calm down rather than as a form of punishment. Think about how you feel when you are upset. Do you always make good decisions? Can you talk calmly about how you feel? Most people need a few minutes to calm down before they can approach a situation rationally. Children are no different.

Time out is simply that—a chance to calm down or to take a break during stressful or frustrating situations. It is most useful as a parenting tool when children are over the age of 3. By that age young children are able to talk and can connect calming down with feeling better. They are also beginning to understand cause and effect, in other words, "When I do this, that happens."

Time out is most useful when your child is so overwhelmed by her emotions, she:

- Could hurt herself or others
- Is destroying property
- Can no longer communicate with you.

Teaching time out

If you are going to use time out, your child needs to learn about it first, before it is needed:

- At a time when you are both calm and not having problems, explain what time out is to your child. Tell him when and why time out will be used in your family. For example, you might say, "Being angry is okay, but hitting is not. If you feel like hitting, you need to calm down. When you feel better, you can tell the person why you are mad."
- Time out should be somewhere where your child feels safe while he gets his emotions under control. Help your child think of things that he can do and where he would like to go to calm down. Your child's ideas may include sitting next to you, going to his room, sitting on his favourite chair or pillow, looking at books, listening to music or hugging a favourite toy. During a time out, it's important for your child to connect calming down with feeling better. Sitting in front of the TV or computer distracts children from how they are feeling, and should not be an option for time out.
- A time out should never be in a place that frightens or humiliates a child, such as a locked room or in a corner facing the wall. If your child is frightened or uncomfortable about being alone, let him know you are close by.
- An alternative is to suggest a time out next to you (sometimes called a time in). Some children find it hard to calm down on their own, and feel better faster when they are close to you. Be kind in letting him know you understand he is upset, and firm in keeping him beside you until he calms down.

- The goal is not to punish—it's to help your child calm down and regain self-control. Tell your child you'll be happy to give him a hug or sit near him if that helps.
- Explain that all people need to take a break to calm down when they are upset. Tell your child that when he's calm and ready to talk (or come back and play without hitting), the time out will end and he can rejoin the activity.

Making time out work

- Don't just threaten to use time out or ask your child if she needs one. Say: "I see you need a time out so you can calm down. When you're ready to talk, you can come back."
- Calmly, but firmly, take your child by the hand and lead her to the time out spot.
- Ignore hollering and yelling, and stay calm.
- Give her a chance to calm down. If your child comes out of the time-out spot while she's still upset, calmly lead her back and repeat: "When you're ready to talk you can come back." You may need to repeat this several times.
- Consistency, calmness and firm kindness are the keys to using time out successfully.
- While your child is taking a time out, use the time to calm yourself. Think of solutions to the problem rather than how bad your child is.
- If your child calms down after a few minutes, the time out is over.

After time out

When your child is ready to talk, use short, simple words he understands to:

- Acknowledge his feelings.
- Describe the behaviour that led to the time out without shaming or blaming.
- Describe how his actions affected others.
- Describe what your child could do instead. For example, "It is okay to be angry. It is not okay to hit your brother. Hitting really hurts. When you are angry, you need to calm down, then you use words to tell your brother you are angry." When your child is older, instead of telling him what to do, you can get him to tell you by saying, "What do you think you could do instead?"

Welcome your child back to the activity or group and drop the subject. If your child needs several time outs in a row, consider changing the activity.

Children do not learn to control themselves as easily when you decide how long they need to be in time out (for example, if you use a timer). They don't learn to connect being able to return to the activity with their own sense of calming down.

You may find your child shows little interest in rejoining you in the activity. During his time out, he may have moved on to something else such as reading or colouring. Don't be concerned that he hasn't been punished. He has settled down and that was the goal.

Keep in mind that you are helping your child develop skills for life. The toddler and preschool years can be a challenge as your child learns how to deal with his emotions, but when he is successful, he:

- Learns to get along with others—both now as a child and later as an adult.
- Develops empathy (understanding the feelings of others).
- Is better able to focus, learn and solve problems.
- Learns ways to calm strong feelings and cope with life's difficult times.

What you can do: taking your own time out

- Take your own time out when stress or frustration overwhelm you to show your child that other people find it useful to calm down before dealing with a problem.

- Make sure your child is safely cared for, and then take a break until you can calmly return to the situation.

- Your child learns a lot by watching you. Be a positive role model. If you deal with anger by yelling or hitting, your child is likely to do the same.

Fears and anxieties

By age 3, many children have overcome some of their earlier fears. They can still develop new fears as they do new things, and as they think and reason in new ways. Preschoolers may be afraid of or anxious about real things such as going to school, moving to a new house, storms or flying in an airplane.

Since preschoolers have such vivid imaginations, they can also fear monsters, ghosts or imaginary animals, or worry about being in a fire or being kidnapped. The most common fears at this age are of animals, the dark and imaginary dangers.

Short separations from you are usually less stressful now. Your child has learned that you still exist even when he can't see you.

Some of the ways to help your preschooler deal with fears include:

- Give her time. Instead of forcing your child to do new things, let her take her own time to try them. She may cling to you until she's comfortable doing things on her own. Once she feels secure, encourage her to try a little more on her own. This same approach can work when helping her with her fears. Go slowly, and stop if your child becomes upset. Never force your child into a situation she fears.

- Give her information. If she's afraid of falling down the toilet or being sucked down the bathtub drain, tell her she's safe and that those things can't happen. Although this logic won't necessarily make the fear go away, it helps her begin to understand.

- Be reassuring. If your child thinks a monster is under the bed or a ghost is in the closet, respect her fear without being overly concerned. Confidently assure your child that there is nothing there, but offer to help her look if she would like. Reassure her that you are close by.

- Listen. Encourage your preschooler to talk about her fears. Let her know everyone is afraid sometimes and that she, like others, can learn to deal with her fears. Remind her about how she got over her previous fears: "Remember when you were little and didn't like going in the swimming pool? And now you're swimming like a fish!"

- Find balance. Being overprotective can make your child afraid to try new things, and overreacting can reinforce fears. Shrugging off your child's fears, on the other hand, can erode her sense of security. Ask yourself if your concerns are justified, make sure to take safety into account, and then let her experience the joy of being successful at something new.

Tattle tales

Tattling (or telling on someone), name-calling and swearing are common in the preschool years. Preschoolers are learning new words and also learning when to use them.

In learning and using words, preschoolers can find themselves in a difficult spot. They are encouraged to give their parents information about all kinds of things, but then told not to tattle. Young preschool children are just learning the difference between right and wrong, and may want to tell you what is going on because they not sure if it's right or wrong.

Your preschooler may also want you to correct another child's behaviour. Unless it is a safety issue, you can respond by confirming your child's concern, saying: "Yes, that is wrong. I'm glad you know that."

As your child gets older, he may be tattling to get you to fix a problem. Preschoolers can learn to solve their own problems, but they need your help. With a sincere voice ask: "That seems to be a problem for you. What do you think you can do about it?" Then help him solve the problem. See *Problem solving* on page 176.

Sometimes, tattling is your child's way of telling you a concern. Your child needs to know he can come to you and other adults for help.

Name-calling often starts when children begin to use words rather than actions when they are angry or frustrated. Unfortunately, they don't always pick the best words and calling someone poo-poo head may be the first thing out of their mouths.

Swearing at this age is often about testing the limits. Deal with it at once. Calmly, but firmly, let your child know you don't like such words, that they are not acceptable, and that you will leave the room if he continues. It is important to follow through if needed. Swearing may seem cute coming from a 4-year-old, but his teachers won't tolerate it once he gets to school. Try not to overreact, as it can make things worse. Set a good example. If you or anyone else uses these words, your preschooler thinks it is okay for him to use them too.

Fantasy and reality

Children 3 to 5 years old start to understand the difference between fantasy and reality, but don't fully know until they're 6 or 7 years old. What parents think of as lying at this stage is often just children telling tall tales or letting their vivid imaginations run wild. Tall tales are perfectly normal at this age.

Your child is not purposefully trying to defy or deceive you. If it is clearly a tall tale, sometimes you can play along with the fantasy; other times you need to bring her back to reality: "Really? I did not see that green dinosaur take your truck. Do you think it might be out in the sandbox?"

Sometimes your child may not tell the truth because she fears being punished. If *stretching the truth* is a problem for your child, you can help by:
- Being honest with others. Your child learns from watching you.
- Not punishing your child for telling the truth. If she says she spilled the milk when trying to pour it and you punish her, she learns that

when she tells the truth, she gets punished, and she will stop telling you the truth. A better solution is to help her clean up, then work together to find a way she can pour milk without spilling it.

- Not setting your child up. For example, when you ask: "Did you break this glass?" when you know she did, you confuse your child. She may want to tell you the truth but be afraid of what might happen. Focus on a solution instead. For example, you could say, "Looks like this glass got broken. Let's get it cleaned up. You get the broom and I'll sweep it up. Next time, please use a plastic glass."

Your preschooler's world

Your preschooler's world is expanding beyond your family. His desire to be with you and to please you remains strong, but he also needs opportunities and encouragement to explore his world and relationships with others. With a growing sense of security that the world is a good place, he feels more comfortable about leaving you for short periods.

Getting along with others

Preschoolers show their growing independence, initiative, capability and creativity by trying new things and making new friends. Some children are quick to do this on their own; others are more comfortable taking their time. Their approach depends a lot on their *temperament* (see page 75). For example, some children scramble up a climbing ladder at the playground; some only try after other children do it.

Preschoolers and play

Play is a more social activity for children in their preschool years. And it's about much more than just having fun. It's through play that children meet other children, make friends and develop thinking and problem-solving skills.

Pretend-play is more elaborate for preschoolers than for toddlers. Preschoolers enjoy acting out roles, such as being a mommy or a daddy, playing house or creating stories with puppets or their toys. Preschoolers like to sing, dance and act out short plays. They like to tell stories.

Playing with others

Preschool children like playing and being with other children and when they do they can learn how to get along with others. At first, children can only see things from their own perspective. They think that everyone else sees or thinks about things the same way they do. Your 4-year-old learns to share and take turns with other children, but can still seem very bossy. Children can understand and follow the rules of simple games, but they often change the rules as they play. When preschoolers play together, they all think that their way is the only right way. They need guidance to learn ways to sort out disagreements.

As preschoolers get older, they have an increasing ability to understand the feelings of others. This is the beginning of empathy.

Boys will be boys and girls will be girls

Many stereotypes about what a boy should be and what a girl should be are now considered old-fashioned beliefs. Not all girls like to wear frilly dresses and not all boys want to play with trucks.

As a rule, however, boys and girls do play differently. Boys are generally more rough-and-tumble when they play, while girls may prefer games with rules, interaction or skills. Girls are more likely to enjoy dramatic, social play such as playing house or dressing up. Boys are more likely to enjoy fantasy play such as being a super hero or a space explorer. No matter what activity your child chooses, encourage all types of play and offer many opportunities for both physical play and pretend-play.

What you can do: to encourage play

- **Make time.** Set aside time each day for your preschooler to choose his own activities and expand his creativity. Give your child the time he needs for play. If possible, try to have play times with other children several times each week.

- **Be ready.** Keep props handy. Dress-up clothes, boxes and play money can all add creativity to pretend play. Make up a box of arts and crafts supplies and set up a special place for creating. Have a special place for displaying creations, and encourage your child to talk about them with grandparents and friends.

- **Make space.** Children need space to play both indoors and out.

- **Inspire imagination.** Create exciting new adventures by reading good books, taking him to the zoo or the museum or watching a movie together. Your child's play is based on his experiences.

- **Help him join in.** If your child is shy or reluctant around other children, you can give him ideas on how to be a part of the group. For example, "Do you want to play firefighters with the other children? If you do, you can go up to them and say 'Can I be a fireman, too?'" or you could say, "This looks like a big fire. I'll help you put it out."

- **Play together.** Try to find some time each day when you can play with your child without distraction. Follow his lead. Let him set the rules as you join him in his fantasy world. Although your preschooler is becoming more independent, and has more skills to draw on, he still needs you and other supportive adults to encourage and promote pretend play. When you play a part in your child's dramatic games and activities, you can lead your child to higher levels of imagination. Also see *Play and Playing* on page 135.

Is your child ready for preschool?

Children between the ages of 3 and 5 are too young for formal grade school, but are often ready for preschool, playschool or nursery school. To decide if your preschooler is ready for these activities, consider whether she:

- Can be away from you for short periods
- Is curious and willing to learn
- Likes to play with other children
- Can stay focused on an activity or story.

If your child still hesitates, you might want to join a parent/tot group so she gets used to being with other children while you're with her. If you choose to send her to preschool, you can help her get used to it by:
- Waiting until she is ready
- Visiting the school
- Meeting the teacher
- Observing the other children
- Pretend-playing school at home
- Volunteering at the school when you can.

Developing positive behaviour

Preschoolers need to be able to explore and be increasingly independent, but they also need to learn and understand that everything has limits, and that includes their behaviour. It is a fine balance that will take several years to learn.

As a parent, it is a balance for you too. If your child faces too many rules, he stops trying to do anything for himself. If he has no limits, he is unable to learn the boundaries of acceptable behaviour. Somewhere in the middle is the best solution. See *Parenting style* on page 9.

Children this age are beginning to understand that their actions have results or consequences, both good and bad. Although they are better at accepting limits, they still need to test them. They can now learn that while a feeling (such as being mad) is acceptable, an action (such as hitting) may not be, and that they can choose a better way (such as using their words) to show emotion. Use these situations to show him how different behaviours lead to different results. This is important for children to learn.

The strategies for teaching your toddler how to behave can still work with your preschooler. See *Getting along with others* on page 142.

Additional suggestions for preschoolers:
- **Give limited choices.** Give your preschooler a more active role in decision-making. Offer choices between two things when you can, but make sure you can live with either choice, for example: "Do you want apple juice or orange juice?" Don't let your child make choices

when none exists. For example, your child must always stay buckled up in the car seat, brush her teeth and go to bed at bedtime, so don't give these as a choice.

- **Encourage capability.** Children need to feel that they are *capable* (are able to do things on their own) and that they are important to other people. Your preschooler is quite capable of many things. At 3 years old, he can help carry light items, or take his dishes to the sink. At 4 years of age, he may be able to sort laundry into dark and light piles, fold socks or help set the table. Find out what your child can do. Have realistic expectations, encourage him to do what he can and let him know he is an important part of your family.
- **Talk about expectations.** Let your preschooler know how you expect him to behave in different situations. If you're going to the grocery store, tell him ahead of time that you're going to buy milk, vegetables and fruit but not candies and treats. Or tell him before you arrive at Grandma's that she doesn't allow running in her house. Help him be successful: let him pick out the apples, avoid going down the candy aisle and keep the shopping trip short. At Grandma's, let him run around the backyard. Be sure to notice and comment on his positive behaviour.
- **Set a good example.** Children learn by seeing, listening and doing. If you want your preschooler to clear his dishes from the table after eating, let him see you take your dishes away and ask him to bring his as well. See *What you can do: take time for teaching* on page 198.
- **Talk about your values.** Talk to your preschooler about what's important to your family. Whether it's respect, honesty, family, fun, learning or politeness, explain why these things are important to your family and culture and how values differ among people and families. Let your child see how you and your family live up to their values.

Dealing with problems

Mistakes are for learning

Everybody makes mistakes and when your child makes one, help him to think of it as a learning opportunity. This is a chance to figure out what to do instead the next time. If the mistake can be fixed, show him how. If you make a mistake, admit it and talk about how you dealt with it.

Natural and logical consequences

Consequences are a natural or logical result of an action. When it's safe, let *natural consequences* occur. Your preschooler can learn that when he doesn't eat, he gets hungry or when he goes out in the rain, he gets wet. At other times, *logical consequences* can follow his actions. Logical consequences are not as obvious as natural consequences, so you may need to point them out.

Consequences are not punishments, they are simply what happens when a behaviour expectation isn't met.

Logical consequences should be *related*, *reasonable* and *respectful*. For example, if he doesn't play safely in the park, take him home, or if his seat belt is undone, the car doesn't move.

Logical consequences are most effective when they directly follow an action. If you tell your child what you expect (for example, he must wear a helmet when riding his tricycle), and he doesn't do it even after a reminder, then follow through. For this example, that would mean putting his tricycle away. This logical consequence is reasonable, related to the behaviour and respects both your child and you. Later, you can let him try again and give him a chance to correct his mistake.

Have patience. Children don't always learn things the first time or right away. Indeed, you can expect your preschooler to ignore or forget much of what you say. You may have to repeat your words and actions many times. When you are calm and consistent in what you do, your child eventually learns. Kindness with firmness, patience and consistency are the foundations of successful parenting.

Problem Solving

Even young children can be very creative when it comes to solving problems, and can work with you to find solutions. If your child is upset over a problem, wait until she is calm to help her (see *Time out* on page 166). Problem solving is a skill your child will use her whole life. The more you help your child solve her own problems now, the better she will resolve conflict later in life.

What you can do: learning to solve problems

These basic steps of the problem-solving process can help you and your child find solutions:

- Acknowledge feelings: "You look mad."
- Accept feelings, but limit actions: "It's okay to be mad. It's not okay to hit. Hitting hurts people."
- Define the problem without blame or judgement: "I see you two girls want to play with the same ball."
- Get suggestions for solutions: "How do you think we could solve this problem so both girls are happy?" Help if needed.
- Together, decide on a solution and try it out.

- Evaluate to see if it has worked. If not, try another solution.
- Notice and comment when you see them getting along.

Sibling rivalry

Sibling rivalry is as old as family life itself. Rivalries and disputes between brothers and sisters can end as quickly as they begin, but can sometimes simmer for hours, days and weeks.

To set the stage for sibling cooperation, you can:
- Make and enforce family rules such as no name-calling or no hitting.
- Avoid labelling your children: "She's always getting into trouble," or "He's just an angel."
- Find a balance between the extremes of treating all your children exactly the same and favouring one over the other. Recognize that each child is unique and what works for one child may not work for another.
- Understand that arguments are normal and that most siblings support each other in situations outside the family.
- Recognize that learning how to fight fairly at home gives them skills for dealing with conflict outside the home.

If your children can't settle their differences and begin to fight:
- Be prepared to step in if things get out of control, for example, if one child is physically or verbally hurting another.
- Separate them and give them both a chance to calm down. Use time out if needed (see *Time out* on page 166). Comfort and reassure a child who is upset or hurt.
- Don't assume you know what happened unless you saw it.

- Once they have calmed down, encourage each child to share her side of the story, without interruption.
- Ask them to come up with a plan that works for both of them. Help with problem solving if needed.

Children and media

Television, videos, DVDs, computers and electronic games play a growing role in our daily lives. Media content has a powerful effect on young children, because they like to be involved with what they see and hear, and can't always tell the difference between make-believe and reality.

Canada's Media Awareness Network offers this advice for the parents of preschool children:

- Start good TV viewing habits before your preschooler starts school. It's harder to influence choices or enforce rules as children get older.
- Limit the time your preschooler spends in front of TVs, computers and video games. The Canadian Paediatric Society advises parents to limit screen time to one hour or less each day for preschoolers and two hours or less for school-aged children.
- Tune into public television. Canadian and American public networks have many quality programs geared to preschoolers.
- Watch TV with your child when you can. Use the opportunity to talk about what she is seeing and understanding. Ask *what* and *how* questions: "What do you think he is going to do?" or "How does that doll work?"
- Turn off shows you find unsuitable or offensive. By making such decisions now, your preschooler is more likely to accept them later.
- Make sure others who care for your preschooler know and follow your TV, computer and video game rules.
- Create a library of favourite shows, movies and games that are appropriate to your child's age and development. Preschoolers love to watch the same shows over and over again—use them as special treats.

Your preschooler won't watch what she can't see. If possible, put the TV and computer in a cabinet or a room where your family spends little time. Use them only when you are together. When your preschooler is little, you control most of the TV/computer time. As she gets older, keep TVs and computers in a central location where they can be seen and used by all. At all ages, keep TVs and computers out of your child's bedroom.

If you're not watching it, turn it off. Make TV viewing special by turning it on for a specific show and turning it off when the show is over. This also sets the stage for good viewing habits in later years.

Adult shows containing sex, violence and swearing are not appropriate for young children. You may think your preschooler doesn't understand, but she is forming images and ideas about how people relate and solve problems, and she may act out or repeat what she sees and hears.

Protecting your preschooler

Preschoolers need the chance to be physically active every day. Physical activity helps them build muscles and coordination, grow their abilities, burn off energy and get fresh air (see *Being active* on page 135).

Preschoolers' adventures can put them in risky situations. They are too young to understand danger and lack the physical and thinking skills to protect themselves. Your child needs to learn and follow your safety rules and you need to enforce those rules, always. Situations involving safety are not a time to offer choices.

While you want to protect your child, you don't want to overprotect him. A safe environment reduces the risk of injury without limiting your child's ability to be physically active.

Children need the freedom and space to develop their gross motor skills, burn off energy and gain a love for active, healthy living. When these things are denied, children face the risk of delayed development, sedentary lifestyle and obesity.

Children need safe surroundings to develop healthy bodies and minds. When they can safely explore, their learning, growth and development can thrive. Active play is an important part of childhood, but getting hurt is not a part of growing up.

Falls

Playgrounds are great places for preschoolers to run and play. Keep in mind a few safety precautions, and let your child enjoy his developing skills.

Preschoolers tend to test the limits of their physical abilities. They might be fearless at the playground, but don't understand falls can results in serious injuries. You can prevent falls by providing constant supervision and safe environments.

Choose playgrounds with a deep soft surface such as sand, pea gravel, wood mulch or a rubber surface underneath the equipment. Grass, soil, shale, concrete and asphalt surfaces do not protect your child from injuries due to falls. Your child may love to climb, but only let her go as high as you can reach. Stand right beside her until she is older and more capable. Most playgrounds have equipment for younger and older children. If your child needs help to climb on a piece of equipment, she is too young for it.

To prevent cuts on feet and to provide the best grip, make sure your child is always wearing shoes with good support.

For a complete checklist, see Alberta Health Services' online *Playground Yes Test.*

Bike safety

Bike riding is a great family outing as most preschoolers enjoy riding on a tricycle or in a bike trailer

Some preschoolers may be able to ride a bicycle, but riding a bicycle in traffic takes a set of physical and mental skills that preschoolers just don't have. Balancing the bike, paying attention to where they are going, watching for cars and road signs—all these things take skill, practice, training and time for normal developmental changes to take place. For most children, that developmental readiness happens gradually between 10 and 14 years of age.

If you think your child is ready for a bicycle, choose a bike that's the right size. Bikes that are too big or too small are a hazard. Have your child sit on the seat. Adjust the seat until his toes can touch the ground on both sides.

Before starting, consider Safe Kids Canada's recommendations:

- Make sure the bike's brakes are working; if there are gears or hand brakes, make sure your child's hands are strong enough to use them
- Check the tires for the right amount of air and that the chain is in place and in good condition
- The bike should have a bell or horn and reflectors
- Use a helmet for every ride
- Young children can ride on sidewalks but must learn to yield to pedestrians

Ride with your child to teach him the safety rules he'll need to know (don't ride on the road, watch out for pedestrians, stop at all stop signs - even when on the sidewalk). Give your child lots of opportunities to learn basic skills before you venture out on the road.

Helmets

By law in Alberta, anyone under the age of 18 must wear a helmet when riding a bicycle, a tricycle or in a bike trailer. Helmets are strongly recommended for adults, too. When you wear your helmet, your child is more likely to accept his. Make bike helmets a habit for the whole family.

Helmets are also recommended for activities such as tobogganing, snow skiing, snowboarding, and ice activities, such as hockey and skating. Use helmets designed specifically for the activity, for example a hockey helmet for hockey and a bike helmet for cycling. Helmets should always be properly fitted and fastened, and always removed before playing on playground equipment.

Healthy outdoor play

Being outside is good for your child; being in direct sunlight isn't. Encourage your child to play in the shade. Use a sunscreen with SPF (sun protection factor) 15 or higher that protects her from both UVA and UVB rays. A wide-brimmed hat shades her face and neck. Avoid being outdoors from mid-morning to mid-afternoon when the sun's rays are the strongest. See *The great outdoors* on page 30 for more information on how to protect your child from the elements.

What you can do: Promoting active safe play

Teach your child to:

- Remove helmets, backpacks and clothing drawstrings before playing
- Keep clear of moving things
- Hold on with both hands when swinging or climbing
- Ride a slide feet first, sitting up, one at a time, and only when it's her turn
- Respect others on the playground—pushing, shoving and tripping can cause injuries
- Keep all ropes away from playground equipment and fences
- Use equipment and toys only as they are meant to be used.

Pedestrian safety

Walking is great exercise. Preschoolers still need to walk with an adult. Children are 9 years old before they can safely cross a street on their own. You can help your preschooler learn the skills he needs, but at this age make sure you (or another adult) are with your child when he crosses a street. Preschoolers are still impulsive. Insist on your child holding your hand when he is near traffic or in a parking lot.

Booster seats

Once a child outgrows a forward-facing car seat, a booster seat is needed because adult seat belts do not fit children properly. Children over 18 kg (40 lbs.) are safest riding in a booster seat in the backseat of your vehicle.

A booster seat is recommended until your child is 9 years old and weighs 36 kg (80 lbs.).

Know how to install and use your child's car seat: First, consult the instructions that come with your child's safety seat and the instructions in your vehicle owner's manual. Next, take the *Booster Seat Yes Test* (available from your community health centre or at www.albertahealthservices.ca). Call Health Link Alberta for information on car seat classes offered in your community or if you have other questions.

Regular checkups

Annual medical checkups are recommended for healthy children. Children should have their vision tested at ages 3 and 6 years. Up-to-date vaccinations protect children from many serious illnesses. For more information, see *Keeping your child healthy* on page 32. Call your public health nurse or Health Link Alberta if you have concerns.

Caring for you

Time

Time not only heals, it can also prevent many problems. Time spent with your child is an investment with many rewards for both of you.

When you make a batch of cookies together or sit down for breakfast with your child, you form important family routines and rituals that help her feel safe and secure. When you go for a 20-minute walk with your preschooler, you create time to talk and be active. When you spend a few minutes snuggling up to read, it's physically comforting and promotes speech and language development.

And when you spend time with your child and your family you show them they are important. To make the most of your time (or find more of it), you can:

- Set priorities and know your limits.
- Focus on what's most important to you. If family is your priority, learn to say no to work, volunteering and other activities.
- Separate your work life from your personal and family life.
- Make flexible work arrangements if you can. Let others know your values and priorities.
- Learn to take care of your personal needs.
- Find activities you can do with your family, such as family nights, walking the dog, kicking a soccer ball, swimming or skating.

Parenting—what's in it for you?

By now, you probably understand why parenting is the most important responsibility you will ever have. No one else can be what you are to your child. Nothing else you do can offer so many lasting rewards.

Being a parent can give you an entirely new way of looking at life. Seeing the world through the eyes of a child is a reminder that innocence exists and hope prevails.

Parenting can also give you a chance to learn more about yourself by looking back at your own childhood, learning from it, and, if you choose, coming to terms with your childhood experiences and lessons. Through parenting you can discover and gain new skills such as patience, humour and creativity. You have a chance to develop a deep and intimate bond with a child. And, of course, your parenting is making a lasting and valuable contribution to society both now and in the future. The value of your role as a parent is beyond measure.

New schoolers
5 TO 6 YEARS

*There is always one moment in childhood when the
door opens and lets the future in.*

—Graham Greene

Growing with your new schooler

As children reach the ages of 5 and 6, they begin to discover the new and
exciting world of school. As they move into the community and make new
relationships, they will better understand the importance of getting along
with others.

We call this period *new school* to mark the most important event of
children this age. This is usually when children begin their formal education.
Some will enter kindergarten or grade school; others will be educated at
home. What's common to all is a strong desire to learn.

New schoolers crave answers and information. They not only ask: "Why?"
but "What if?" This is a time of transition for children. Even if they are used
to going to day care or preschool, starting school is a big step.

Your new schooler's body

Your new schooler will continue to grow at his own rate, which can be
different from his brothers, sisters, friends and classmates. He will grow in
spurts; he will seem to stay the same size for weeks, then almost overnight
appear taller. As his body fills out, he will grow stronger and will want to test
his new-found abilities.

Children this age are increasingly coordinated and now enjoy games that
need more physical skill, such as tag, hide and seek, and hopscotch. They like
to hop, skip and jump, and are ready to learn how to ride a bicycle, with your
help and the right equipment. For some children, this is a good time to

introduce them to sports such as soccer, hockey, golf and swimming. At this age, it's important to keep the focus on participating rather than competing.

Although confident of their physical abilities, new schoolers may think they can do more than they can. They need to learn safe limits.

As the fine motor skills of new schoolers improve, they can learn to tie their shoelaces and use a fork and knife when eating. Their drawings become more detailed and they add bodies, arms, legs, feet, arms and face to pictures of people. They can usually print their own name and simple words, although they may use creative spelling.

New schoolers can dress and undress themselves, but they may dawdle or take their time. By 6 years old, your new schooler probably starts to have definite ideas about the clothes she wants to wear. Her likes and dislikes are often influenced by what others wear and she may change her mind from week to week. You still need to remind your new schooler regularly to wash her hands and clean her face, neck and body when bathing or showering.

Growing pains

Many children in elementary school experience *growing pains* in their legs. Why children feel these pains is largely a mystery, although children most often have them at bedtime during a growth spurt.

Growing pains are felt in the leg muscles—not the joints. They are generally not a cause for concern and are usually gone by morning. To ease the pain, you can try gently rubbing your child's legs. If the pain seems constant or in the joints, or if you are concerned, check with your doctor.

Eating

When children are in school, they are not as physically active, but they still need nutritious food for the enormous increase in their brainwork. New schoolers' appetites go up and down, but it's still important to feed them a variety of food recommended by Canada's Food Guide. New schoolers continue to need frequent refuelling, so pack a nutritious snack for recess. They'll need it.

Breakfast makes champions

Breakfast is essential for your child to be successful at school. A child cannot learn if she is hungry. If your child doesn't like to eat in the morning, look at what else is going on:

- Is your morning too rushed?
- Is she too busy watching her favourite TV show?
- Is she getting enough sleep?
- Is she bored with eating the same thing day after day?

Talk to your public health nurse or call Health Link Alberta for ideas and suggestions on healthy breakfasts. If getting enough food is a problem for your family, talk to your school principal or public health nurse; they can help.

Eating lunches at school

For many children, going to school means eating lunch at school. Like school itself, this may be something your new schooler needs to get used to. He may find lunchtime too busy, exciting or stressful to focus on eating. Five- and 6-year-old children can still be picky eaters and without an adult to encourage them, they may eat only part of their lunch.

To make sure your child gets the food he needs you can:

- Pack a variety of foods for lunch and have a small snack ready for after school.
- Pack smaller portions of food in separate containers so your child can eat some at recess and some at lunch.
- Encourage him to help make and pack his lunch. He may take more interest in something he has made himself.
- Try to maintain a three-meal and three-snack schedule on the weekend as well, so your child gets used to having food at regular times.
- Send hot or cold foods in a Thermos or insulated container.
- Ask your child to bring uneaten food home so you can keep track of what he is eating.
- Check the school's policies about the types of food children can bring to school and when they can eat.

If you are concerned that your child is not eating at school, check with your school to see if (and what) he is eating.

Teeth and oral health

Between the ages of 5 and 8, children begin to lose their baby teeth. Their permanent teeth will grow in over the next few years. A child usually has most of her permanent teeth by the age of 13, except her wisdom teeth, which usually grow in after the age of 17.

Continue to help your child brush and floss her teeth until she is 8 years old (for more information, see *How to brush* on page 124 and *Using dental floss*, page 99).

Injured teeth

New schoolers are active and adventurous and this increases their chances of tooth injuries. If your child injures, breaks or knocks out a tooth, take him and the tooth to the dentist right away. When your child starts contact sports, use a mouthguard to protect his teeth from injury. Your dentist can recommend the right mouthguard for your child.

Sealants

Sealants are an effective way to protect teeth from cavities. They are thin plastic coatings painted on the chewing surfaces of healthy molars (back teeth). The chewing surfaces of the back teeth are rough and uneven, and have small pits and grooves, which are difficult to clean with a toothbrush.

Sealants help keep out the germs and food that cause cavities. Permanent molars can be sealed as soon as they come in (between the ages of 5 and 7, and 11 and 14). While sealants protect part of the tooth, good dental habits are still needed for a healthy mouth and teeth.

If you have questions about sealants, talk to your dentist or call Health Link Alberta.

Sleeping

School is hard work for children and it can leave them very tired as they get used to being in a classroom for the whole day. Getting a good sleep every night can help your child adjust.

Children need sleep to restore their energy and to help them focus and concentrate on learning. *Sleep deprivation* (not getting enough sleep) leads to a temporary loss of IQ levels, reasoning and memory. It can affect children's behaviour. When children don't get enough sleep on a regular basis, all aspects of their life can be affected.

If your child is having trouble getting used to the demands of school, try putting her to bed a half-hour or hour earlier than normal for a week and see how she responds. Most school-aged children need about 10 hours of sleep a night. Late nights and school days don't mix.

Toilet teaching

Your child is likely able to get to the bathroom on his own by now, but some children don't like to use the toilet when they're away from home. They may feel uncomfortable using public washrooms.

If you find your child unable to use the toilet away from home, bring the topic up with your child's caregiver, teacher or principal to make sure your child has nothing to fear. Work with your child to deal with any issues, reassuring her and teaching her how to ask other adults for help.

Wherever and whenever your child uses the toilet, remind her to wash her hands well.

Your new schooler's mind

By the time they are 5 years old, children's identities have begun to form. Their sense of who they are gets stronger and their pretend play becomes more complex and based on themes. As children try out new roles, they learn more about themselves and more about being a boy or girl.

Industry is the developmental task of 6- to 12-year-olds. You will see it emerge in your 6-year-old as she eagerly starts and finishes projects and activities. New schoolers take great pride in what they can do, but can also feel frustrated, embarrassed or ashamed if they are not able to do things as well as they or others would like. Your child continues to need your love, support and trust in order to feel good about herself.

Eager to learn, meet new people and do new things, new schoolers are increasingly ready to leave their parents' side for longer and longer periods. When your child enters elementary school, those periods stretch from a few hours to most of a day.

This emotional independence is a big step and something that can be a difficult adjustment for both of you. Starting school can be stressful for some children. Every child reacts to this change in her own way. Your child may cling to you, be angry, argue with you or she may just say, "Bye, Dad," and skip off to join her new friends without looking back. When you understand your child's temperament (see page 75) you can better know what to expect.

Most children this age feel quite protective of their belongings and their privacy. New schoolers are able to share, but they may choose, at times, to keep some things (like their toys, books or thoughts) just to themselves.

Your child still needs your encouragement and for you to set limits while she learns to do more and more for herself and by herself.

Being apart for longer periods is a big adjustment for parents as well. No longer are you in control of everything your child does or who influences her. Of course, you'll want to know about your child's day, but insisting on learning every detail can make your child less likely to want to talk about it.

Speech and language in the new school years

Children need language to let others know what they need and want—especially as they make new relationships. While you may understand that your child's raised brow means he doesn't understand something or his tapping foot means he's bored, people outside your immediate family may not. Of course, language is also essential for reading and writing, which are the foundation of all academic learning.

Understanding typical speech and language development helps you know what to expect and when to seek help.

At 5 years old, new schoolers:

- Are understood by others
- Say most speech sounds correctly
- Talk for fun, friendship or to achieve a purpose
- Understand humour and usually know when people are joking
- Enjoy listening to books of all kinds, such as alphabet books, fairy tales and rhyming stories
- Know the meaning of simple words
- May ask about abstract words or concepts, such as science, electricity or "Why is the sky blue?"
- Can understand and talk about stories, songs and shows on television
- Like to use new words.

If, at 5 years old, your new schooler is hard to understand, does not speak in complete sentences or cannot follow directions, his language and speech should be assessed. Talk to your child's teacher, doctor or public health nurse or call Health Link Alberta for more information about speech pathology services in your area.

At 6 years old, new schoolers:

- Can talk in complete sentences although they may run together
- Use the past, present and future forms of words correctly
- Like to talk with and about friends and family
- Can think of ideas for solving problems
- Use good grammar
- Are able to say most speech sounds correctly
- Begin to understand the time concepts of days, weeks and seasons
- Start to write and recognize written words

Continue to inspire your new schooler's language development. Nurturing language in your child is one of the best ways of encouraging a passion for lifelong learning.

What you can do: encouraging language in your new schooler

- Encourage your child to talk about her feelings, thoughts, hopes and fears.
- Show your interest by taking the time to really listen.
- Talk to your child in the same tone of voice that you would use with your best friend.
- Encourage exploration and explain how things work.
- Look at family photos and keepsakes. Share stories about family history and events.
- Sing songs. Play word games. Make up rhymes. Listen to music.
- Encourage your child to write and ask her to read it to you. Don't worry about correct spelling at this age.
- Tap into your child's interests to get her excited about reading: read the sports section together, find books about something she likes, or look for children's magazines at the library.
- Keep reading together even as your child learns to read by herself. Make reading something your whole family does.
- Be patient. Reading and writing are complex skills that take time to learn.

Feelings and emotions

New schoolers are better able to control and express their emotions than when they were younger, but they may still struggle to find the exact words to describe their feelings. They are familiar with the four main feelings (sad, mad, happy and scared) and will continue to experience an ever-widening range of emotions (such as jealousy, shame, embarrassment, and love). Children this age are less likely to respond physically to their emotions. By now, they should be able to use words and gestures instead to describe how they are feeling—at least most of the time.

Sometimes people experience two feelings at the same time. Your child may be quite confused the first few times she has mixed emotions. Help her learn that she can feel, and deal with, two things at once (such as excited and scared, or happy and sad) by talking about the experience and giving the emotions a name.

As their skills with problem-solving improve, new schoolers can learn to use self-talk to calm themselves (for example: "I need to calm down. Take some deep breaths. What else can I do to feel better?"). Encourage this behaviour with your child—it helps her form healthy mental thoughts and actions.

By 5 years old, many children start to understand and share the feelings of anger, sadness and joy in others. As they recognize these feelings in family and friends, they may respond and offer comfort. Look for opportunities to support and teach these feelings and actions. Children who develop this skill (known as empathy) have much healthier relationships, both as children and as adults.

No child can be in control all the time, and your child can still become overwhelmed and frustrated. She may find it hard to laugh at herself and may be easily embarrassed. Children this age don't like to be corrected and can be very hurt when someone is angry with them.

Continue to acknowledge and accept your child's feelings even as you help her change her behaviour. It's important that she knows her feelings are real and acceptable, even if her behaviour is not.

By this age, tantrums should be a rare and something caused only by extreme frustration or disappointment. If you child is having more tantrums, or if they are violent or destructive, talk to your doctor or public health nurse to get help for your child and coping strategies for you.

Fears

While fears are generally less of a problem in new schoolers, fear of the dark, the imaginary (monsters and ghosts) and animals can still be a problem. As children understand the realities of life and death, new fears may be felt—for example, fear of a loved one dying or fear of strangers or burglars. Listen to your child's fears.

Show empathy and calm, matter-of-fact reassurance. Don't dismiss your child's fears, but don't make a big fuss either. Never make fun of or shame your child. Be supportive and remind him how he has overcome other fears in the past.

While fears can be common at this age, fears sometimes arise from real events. Look for any underlying causes. If fears overwhelm your child, get professional help.

Nervous habits

Nervous habits such as biting nails, twisting hair, tugging ears and grinding teeth can be signs of stress. Adjusting to new routines, fear of disapproval, moving or making new friends can all cause stress in children.

Responding calmly and positively to your child's nervous habits helps her overcome and eventually stop them. Children punished for their habits can end up feeling more stress and a greater need for comfort, making their habits worse.

As your child learns to cope with stress or learns other ways to comfort herself, her nervous habit may just disappear.

What you can do: breaking nervous habits

- Spend more time with your child and give her positive attention.
- Try to find and reduce the stresses in your child's life that may be causing the habit.
- Make sure she gets enough sleep and healthy food.
- Offer a replacement such as a worry stone, doll or lucky charm she can rub, or an elastic she can stretch. Favourite and familiar objects, such as blankets, stuffed toys or pictures, can help your child feel more comfortable.
- Find some quiet time to spend alone (for example, on a walk or just before bed) to talk about her day and how she is feeling.
- Let her know most people find it hard to make changes. Remind her of other times when she was successful in making changes and dealing with stress.
- Help your child come up with her own ideas for dealing with her stresses and fears.

If your child's nervous habits are becoming compulsive or interfering with her daily life, talk to your doctor.

New Schoolers

Your new schooler's world

At the ages of 5 and 6, your child is meeting new people and going new places, often through kindergarten and school. Her world is bigger than ever and as she discovers everything about it, she is away from you more. As this happens, she needs to learn to feel comfortable and confident on her own, with groups of other children and in new environments, such as busy playgrounds and classrooms.

Getting along with others

At 5 years old, children often feel good about themselves. They are typically friendly and for the most part, easy to get along with. New schoolers like to please the important adults in their lives and are often eager to help. They enjoy group games and activities with others.

These activities create new relationships and bring about a whole new set of things to learn. New schoolers are much more aware of the personal power they hold in a relationship and use it to test their ability to make things happen. Some children are physical. They can use this to deal with stress by burning off energy, but it can sometimes lead to aggression or rough play. Other children are verbal and while they can learn to be great at reasoning and negotiating, they can also use their words to exclude others.

The parents of new schoolers need to be understanding but firm. New schoolers are learning the boundaries of behaviour and they need their parents' help as they learn to get along with others. When wisely guided through this stage, children learn that their behaviour has its own consequences. If they are rough or mean, their friends won't want to play with them. They can learn better ways to get along and express their feelings.

Children's social networks often grow when they start school. Even children who have been in daycare and preschool enter a newer, bigger world in school. School life often has many new and different rules than at home or at a daycare or day home.

Ready for school?

Depending on where you live and your child's readiness, he can start kindergarten as early as 4-1/2 years old, but most children start when they are 5.

If you are trying to decide if your child is ready for school, consider the following:

• The length of time your child is able to be away from you.
• His experience in a daycare, day home, nursery or preschool setting.

- His ability to use the washroom and do simple tasks for himself (such as putting on and taking off his own coat, hat, mitts, boots and shoes).
- Your child's ability to focus and pay attention.
- How well he gets along with other children.
- How well he gets along with and takes direction from other adults.

If your child seems academically but not socially ready for kindergarten, you may want to consider other options such as preschool, day camps and play groups.

Think about what it means to your child's future. Children who are bright and eager to go to school at an early age can struggle socially and emotionally as teens when they are a year younger than their peers. This is difficult to predict, but worth thinking about, as differences in maturity can be more noticeable as your child gets older.

What you can do: getting ready for school

- Take your child for a health checkup. Physical checkups (including medical, dental, vision and hearing) and up-to-date vaccinations promote a healthy start for school and can identify potential health problems early before they cause learning delays (see *Regular checkups* on page 34).
- Talk about the change. Explain what will be the same and what will be different. Talk about what he can expect at school and what you will do when he is not with you.
- Take a school tour so he can meet his teacher and see the classroom, washroom, library, gym and playground.
- Look for a friend. Try to remember the names of one or two other children. Having a friend means your child doesn't have to feel alone.
- Read books on starting school. Local libraries have many titles.
- Respect your child's temperament (see page 75). Children adjust to change in different ways.
- Be enthusiastic. Your child is entering a new stage of life and is having many new experiences. Share his excitement!

Learning from a new teacher

While you continue to be your child's most caring and influential teacher, his schoolteachers soon become very important people in his life too. You can get to know your child's teacher through regular contact. This also gives the teachers a chance to talk about how your child acts with other children and how he is doing with his studies.

New schoolers often enjoy sharing their schoolwork with their family. They take great pride in what they've created and feel honoured when it's posted on the bulletin board or refrigerator. The first time they read to you is a moment to treasure forever.

Keep your child's enthusiasm and excitement for learning alive by handing out compliments and avoiding criticism. Put more emphasis on the effort than on a perfect final product. Encourage your child to think by asking, "What do you think about that?" or "I wonder why that happened?" rather than giving answers right away.

Remember, a school day is very long for 5- or 6-year-old children. The morning's activities are a distant memory by the time they see you after school. One way to encourage your child to talk about his day is to ask a couple of specific questions about his activities. Rather than asking, "How was school?" ask, "Who did you sit with at lunch today?" or "What book did Mr. Smith read to you today?"

Create an area at home for your child's school books and spend a few minutes every day talking about his day. Showing your interest will help him feel he is doing something interesting and important—which is exactly what learning is.

Finding time

Once children begin school, their days are much busier, yet often much less active. Finding time for active play is important, as active children learn better, are healthier and are more likely to be active as adults. Physical activity can be inexpensive and easy—as simple as a walk to the park or a bike ride after supper.

It's important, however, not to schedule every waking minute of a child's day with school, activities and appointments. Children who learn to entertain themselves for part of their day become more self-reliant. To a child, unscheduled time is a chance for her to find things she likes to do, such as reading, painting, playing with a nearby friend or spending time with you. Try to encourage your child's interests so she doesn't always turn to the TV or computer when she is bored. (Also see *Children and media* on page 178).

Try to find a few minutes each day for your child to share her day with you. When your new schooler knows that her secure base is still there, she will feel safe in exploring her wide new world.

Organized activities like preschool, daycare and school require children to have a different level of attention. Their day may be more structured than they are used to at home. Once she starts school, your young child spends a lot of energy staying focused. She needs "down time" once she gets home to burn off some physical energy and reconnect with the ones she loves.

"I don't like school!"

Children sometimes get tired of school once the novelty wears off. Your child may have separation anxiety if she is not used to being away from you. She may want to spend more time with you. She may be just plain tired.

Some suggestions for helping your child cope:

- Make sure she has enough sleep and good food.
- Try not to over-schedule activities. Your child is spending lots of energy just staying alert and focused for the day.
- Set aside or increase the special or one-on-one time you spend together.

If your child really resists going to school or complains of constant stomach aches or headaches, it may be more serious. Talk to the teacher and ask how your child is getting along with others and adjusting to school life. Speak to other parents to see if their children have similar problems. Have a checkup with your family doctor to rule out physical causes.

Listen to your child. Try to understand what she might be feeling and help her think of solutions.

If your child does not get along with her teacher, speak honestly to both about it. Avoid blame and work on finding a solution that works for everyone. If you are unable to find a solution, ask the principal to help you settle the issue.

Helping out at home

Simple chores help new schoolers learn that everyone has an important role in making family life run smoothly. Children don't always do their chores exactly the way their parents do, but it's the effort that counts. With time and practice, their skills improve. Giving your child chores suited to her age helps her feel she belongs and is capable—two of the most important ingredients for a healthy self-esteem.

■■■■■■■■■■■■■■■■■■■■■■■■■■■■■■■■■■■■■

What you can do: take time for teaching

Take the time to teach your child skills such as
household chores. Break the task down into small steps.
Cheryl Erwin, co-author of several books on positive
discipline, suggests four steps to gradually build skills
with young children:

1. You do it, they watch.
2. You do it, they help.
3. They do it, you help.
4. They do it, you watch.

■■■■■■■■■■■■■■■■■■■■■■■■■■■■■■■■■■■■■

Play

For new schoolers, play becomes a very social activity. They love to play with
friends and it is through this play that they learn about themselves, others and
how to get along.

Pretend play is much more complex now and tends to be based on themes
such as popular stories, TV shows, superheroes or social roles. Puppet shows
and play-acting are popular as children try out these new roles, take on other's
thoughts, and learn to cope with their emotions. At this stage, boys tend to
prefer to play with boys, and girls with girls.

Six-year-olds can be full of contradictions. They often seek approval and
attention and are eager to please—then just as likely to be stubborn and bossy.
Six-year-olds are very concrete thinkers (something is either right or it's
wrong, there is nothing in between). They are very quick to point out when
another child misbehaves and, although they like to be treated fairly, may
have quite strict rules about what another child can or cannot do when
they play.

Children this age like games with rules, although they may still find it hard
to always follow them. Some children simply quit playing if things don't go
their way or think others are being unfair. Learning to play by the rules
takes time.

New schoolers love to be active and play games involving physical skill.
At this stage, physical activity is best if it is non-competitive. This gives
children the chance to develop skills without the fear of failure or not being
good enough.

Making friends

New schoolers love to be with their friends. Having friends, however, seems inevitably to lead to the occasional disagreements and fights. Your 5-year-old wants to set the rules, so does his best friend—and the fight is on. New schoolers can learn negotiating skills, but may need your help at first.

Encourage your child to use his problem solving skills (see page 176). Try not to rush in and fix all their problems for them or involve other parents (unless it is truly serious). A wise grandmother once said, "The children will get over it long before the parents will." Let the children know you are confident they can work things out so that everyone is happy and that you are available if they need help.

What you can do: getting along with friends

Learning to get along with others is not always easy. You can help your child and her young friends get along by:

- Explaining your family's guidelines and expectations when friends are over to play. Children this age don't need hands-on supervision, but they need to know a caring adult is close by.
- Consistently enforcing the limits with kind firmness and problem solving (see page 176).
- Focusing on solutions instead of blame. Help them come up with ideas for settling arguments.
- Complimenting them when they are getting along with each other.
- Setting a good example. Children learn what they live.
- Teaching children respect by treating them (and others) with respect.
- Limiting and monitoring TV, video and computer time. Children are affected by the violence they see in the media.

Bullying and teasing

Bullying and teasing are, sadly, something almost every boy and girl will have to deal with at some time. By knowing the signs of bullying and how to deal with it, you can help stop bullying in its tracks.

Bullying does not have to be physical for a child to be deeply hurt. Name-calling, threats, mean-spirited gossip and even cruel jokes can all harm a child's sense of security and self-esteem.

Your child may be afraid to tell you that he's being bullied or teased, but other signs may point to the trauma he's facing. He may:

- Not want to go to school
- Ask to go to school late and come home early
- Say he has a headache or stomach ache
- Have things he owns go missing
- Seem always worried or afraid about going to school
- Suddenly lose a circle of friends
- Be distracted or unable to concentrate on school work or other activities.

What you can do: if your child is bullied

If he says he's being bullied or teased, believe him and listen carefully. When dealing with bullying, it's helpful to:

- Control your own emotions. Overreacting can make your child feel he's done something wrong.
- Let your child know that you believe him, you'll support him and you'll work with the school to protect him.
- Assure your child that no one has the right to bully another person.
- Help your child develop strategies for dealing with bullies.
- Work closely with a schoolteacher or principal to find solutions to stop the bullying or teasing.

If your child bullies

If your child bullies and teases other children, you need to take positive action right away. If not stopped, bullies become more aggressive.

Work with her teacher or principal to develop a plan. Punishing a child for bullying usually leads to more problems. Instead, make sure your child apologizes to the bullied child and arrange for her to fix or replace what she destroyed. Make sure your child knows you are there for her. Be clear that you will not fix the problem for her but you will help her make things right. She needs to assume responsibility and figure out how to keep it from happening again.

At home and at school, let your child know what's acceptable and what's not. Keep rules simple, to a minimum and ensure they apply to everyone. Be very clear about your expectations for her behaviour. When there is a problem, let her know in clear, uncertain terms. Kindly and firmly follow through with your limits. Focus on solutions, not blame and be consistent.

What you can do: if your child bullies

If your child is bullying others, you can:

- Set firm limits and clear expectations of behaviour. Help your child to understand that she can control and choose how she behaves.

- Find chances for her to behave in caring and helpful ways both at school and in other areas of her life.

- Set good examples for caring, respectful relationships at home and with others.

- Give your child love and attention. Some aggressive children see the world as a hostile place. They think: "I'll hit before someone hits me." Acknowledging and encouraging positive behaviour increases your child's self-esteem and helps her see the world as a more positive place.

- Monitor and limit TV and electronic games—not as a punishment, but as a way to control the effects of exposure to violent behaviour. Help your child find other activities she can enjoy.

- Give your child chances to be active—outside with you, or in organized activities or sports.

- Teach your child problem-solving (see page 176).

Protecting your new schooler

As your child moves into the expanded world of friends and school, he won't always have you close by. Like children of all ages, new schoolers need to be active for healthy growth and development. They need to be supervised by a responsible adult whether at school or in the playground, but not as closely as when they were toddlers. New schoolers need a little more freedom to explore along with rules on how to stay safe.

New schoolers, like younger children, are still too young to realize all the dangers around them or how to completely protect themselves. They are starting to remember simple safety rules but when excited they may not always follow them. Frequently remind your child of your safety rules and enforce those rules, always. Situations involving safety are not a time to offer choices—at any age.

Playground safety

Falls off playground equipment are a leading cause of injury among children 5 to 9 years of age. Help your child be safe by teaching simple safety rules:
- Always wear shoes.
- Take turns.
- Keep clear of moving things. Keep all ropes away from playground equipment and fences.
- Hold on with both hands when swinging or climbing. Slide down feet first, sitting up and one person at a time.
- Use equipment and toys as they are meant to be used.
- Play fair—no pushing, shoving or tripping.

Bike safety

Your new schooler may soon be riding a two-wheeled bike. Once he can stay upright, help him understand how to ride safely (where to ride, signaling, braking, passing pedestrians and road safety) and that bikes and helmets always go together (indeed, it's the law in Alberta).

Safe Kids Canada reminds parents that riding a bike safely in traffic takes a complex set of skills which develop gradually over time. Children under the age of 9 should always ride with an adult, even if they take the same route (between home and school) several times a week. Riding to and from school with your child is a great way to be active together and to teach your child the rules of the road. Also see *Bike safety* on page 179.

Walking to school

Walking to school is great exercise, but new schoolers still need to do this with an adult. Children are 9 years old before they have all the skills they need to safely cross a street on their own. You can help your preschooler learn these skills, but at this age make sure you (or another adult or crosswalk guard) are with your child when she crosses a street. Your child may no longer want to hold your hand when walking, but she needs to learn to stay close to you in traffic, when crossing roads and in parking lots.

Booster seats

Once a child outgrows a forward-facing car seat, a booster seat is needed. Adult seat belts do not fit children properly and can cause very serious injuries in a crash or sudden stop. Children over 18 kg (40 lbs.) are safest riding in a booster seat in the backseat of your vehicle. A booster seat is recommended until your child is 9 years old and weighs 36 kg (80 lbs.).

Know how to install and use your child's booster seat: First, consult the instructions that come with your child's safety seat and the instructions in your vehicle owner's manual. Next, take the *Booster Seat Yes Test* (available from your community health centre or at www.albertahealthservices.ca). Call Health Link Alberta for information on car seat classes offered in your community or if you have other questions.

Fires

Your child is taught how to respond to fires through fire drills at school and it is a good idea for you to practise them at home as a family as well. That way, your child can also learn how to get out of the house in case of a fire. Teach your child to:
- Get low and go; crawl along the floor to stay below the smoke
- Stop, drop and roll if his clothes catch fire
- Follow your family's fire plan, and safely climb out of a window.

Have smoke detectors in your home and check them every month to make sure they are working.

Internet safety

If your child uses the Internet, move your computer to a central location and monitor and guide his "surfing." This sets the tone for how he explores in the years ahead. The Canadian Paediatric Society recommends that parents do not put Internet-connected computers, TV's or video games in a child's bedroom. Keep them in areas where everyone has access.

Sun protection

Being outside is good for your child; being in direct sunlight isn't. Use a sunscreen with SPF (sun protection factor) of 15 or higher that protects against both UVA and UVB rays. Apply sunscreen before your child leaves for school and make sure he has extra in his backpack if going on a field trip. A wide-brimmed hat shades the face and neck—keep one in your child's backpack so he has one to wear at recess.

Whether at home or school, encourage your child to play in the shade, staying out of direct sunlight whenever possible. See *The great outdoors* on page 30 for more information on how to protect your child from the elements.

Regular checkups

Continue to guard your child's health with regular checkups and routine vaccinations. For more information on keeping children healthy and safe at any age, see *Protecting your child* on page 26 and *Keeping your child healthy* on page 32.

Caring for you

How quickly the years fly by. As your child begins school, you may struggle with her growing independence and being separated from her. You may think: "She'll never be able to eat her lunch without me!" or "Taking the bus is far too grown-up for her," or "How will she ever find the washroom?" It may seem hard to believe at first, but your child will learn to do all these things.

Realizing that your child can get along at school just fine without you is not always easy for a parent. But you do get used to your child going to school.

As your child enters this new world, her independence grows and she may challenge you more, listen to you less and be influenced greatly by teachers and friends. She tests and explores her new independence in many ways, and may even question you about your family's traditions, habits and values. This is part of her discovery of this new part of herself. She is learning about a broader world and her place in it.

As your child changes, you do too. As a parent, you've been a comforter, protector, nurturer and teacher. Now you also become an advocate, cheerleader, coach and counsellor. With your child in school, you won't be there to fix all her problems. She needs to learn to think for herself and learn how to solve her own problems. The loving guidance you have given her has helped build these skills and set the stage for her to be successful. She will still need your support. Let her know that if she needs you, you are there for her.

Be your child's biggest supporter. Talk to her about her interests, meet her friends and introduce yourself to her teacher, the school secretary and principal. This is not always easy if you are shy or if English is not your first language. Start small—just saying hello to another parent in the playground can be a start.

Elementary schools encourage and value parent participation. Be active in your child's school in whatever way you can. Whether volunteering for field trips, attending school assemblies and concerts or sitting on the school council, your interest shows your child that her learning is important to you. When you're involved in your child's learning, your child is more likely to succeed.

While your child may stray from you at times, she will return. Children still very much need the comfort, patience, direction and wisdom of their parents as they enter the middle years of childhood. Even as their peers take on a greater influence, you will always be the most influential person in your child's life.

You do not become less of a parent as your child grows up. Your child will need your support and encouragement through all the different phases and stages of her life. Parenting will be rewarding, demanding, challenging and joyous through all of them. Continue to expand your parenting skills. Remember, parenting programs are for everyone and at any stage of parenting. They are a great way to meet other parents who are having similar experiences and to develop new skills for building and strengthening your relationship with your child.

With the foundation years of early childhood behind you, our hope is for both you and your child to continue growing, loving and learning together.

Index

Index

Important Phone Numbers
Emergency 9-1-1

Alberta Poison Centre Calgary 403-944-1414

or call toll free 1-800-332-1414

Child Abuse Hotline 1-800-387-KIDS (5437)

Health Link Alberta

Calgary and area: 403-943-LINK (5465)

Edmonton and area: 780-408-LINK (5465)

Or call Toll-free: 1-866-408-LINK (5465)

Early Start Line (up to 2 months) 403-244-8351

Medication and Herbal Advice 1-888-944-1012

Child Disability Resource Link 1-866-346-4661

Family Violence Information Line 310-1818

Community Services and Resources 2-1-1

Family Doctor: _____

Pediatrician: _____

Dentist: _____

Optometrist: _____

Community Health Centre: _____

Child Care: _____

People I can call for support: _____

_____

Alberta Health Care Numbers:

Name _____ Number _____

Name _____ Number _____

Name _____ Number _____

Name _____ Number _____

Name _____ Number _____